The Peninsular War
Wellington's Battlefields Revisited

First published in Great Britain in 2010

Reprinted in 2011 by
Pen & Sword Military
an imprint of
Pen & Sword Books Ltd
47 Church Street
Barnsley
South Yorkshire
S70 2AS

Opposite, a view from the French defences on the Lesser Rhune. In the distance can be seen the star fort on the Mouiz plateau. Both positions were taken by the Light Division during the Battle of the Nivelle on 10 November 1813.

ISBN 978-1-84884-529-9

A CIP catalogue record for this book is available from the British Library.

Typeset in 11pt Ehrhardt by
Mac Style, Beverley, E. Yorkshire

Printed and bound in India by Replika Press Pvt. Ltd.

Pen & Sword Books Ltd incorporates the Imprints of Pen & Sword Aviation, Pen & Sword Family History, Pen & Sword Maritime, Pen & Sword Military, Pen & Sword Discovery, Wharncliffe Local History, Wharncliffe True Crime, Wharncliffe Transport, Pen & Sword Select, Pen & Sword Military Classics, Leo Cooper, The Praetorian Press, Remember When, Seaforth Publishing and Frontline Publishing.

For a complete list of Pen & Sword titles please contact
PEN & SWORD BOOKS LIMITED
47 Church Street, Barnsley, South Yorkshire, S70 2AS, England
E-mail: enquiries@pen-and-sword.co.uk
Website: www.pen-and-sword.co.uk

The Peninsular War
Wellington's Battlefields Revisited

Pen & Sword
MILITARY

Wellington: An Introduction

When the British army under Lieutenant General Sir Arthur Wellesley landed in Portugal in August 1808, few could have imagined the impact that the thirty-nine-year-old commander and his soldiers would make on European history. Britain at the time had a less than glorious recent military record, with only one minor success over the French at Maida in southern Italy in July 1806. Although her navy had destroyed the French and Spanish fleets at Trafalgar in October 1805, her army had been humiliated in Egypt in 1807 when an attempt to oust the pro-French ruler Muhammad Ali had ended in disaster. Equally calamitous had been an attempt to establish a British foothold in South America, where the lure of gold and silver, and rumours that the Spanish colonies of Buenos Aires and Montevideo were preparing to secede, had prompted an expedition led by Brigadier William Carr Beresford to occupy Buenos Aires in June 1806, only for it to be forced to surrender by local militia and Spanish regulars. While Montevideo was successfully occupied, a further attack on Buenos Aires in July 1807 failed disastrously: over two thousand men were lost, the majority taken prisoner, including officers like Robert Craufurd and Denis Pack who were subsequently to distinguish themselves in the Peninsula. It is one of the great might-have-beens of history that Wellesley was in fact planning another expedition to the Rio de la Plata when, in June 1808, the British government asked him to take command of the forces they had recently decided to send to Portugal to face the French armies occupying the Peninsula.

By the summer of 1808 Napoleon Bonaparte was the scourge of all Europe. Crushing victories against the Austrians under Mack at Ulm and an Austro-Russian army at Austerlitz towards the end of 1805 had brought about the collapse of the Third Coalition (comprising Britain, Austria, Russia, Sweden, Naples and some German states) against France. Extensively reorganised by Napoleon, the French army which had won him his supremacy was a formidable military machine. The élite Imperial Guard was feared throughout Europe, and the cavalry – kept supplied with horses from occupied countries – had a daunting reputation. It was an army that had become used to living off the land, a considerable advantage over opponents who depended on slow-moving supply wagons, and it was commanded by generals who could boast a wealth of battlefield experience. Its one weakness, perhaps, was Napoleon's determination to retain a monopoly of authority. He had personally led most of his armies in the field and was reluctant to concede operational control to his marshals, who were therefore unused to making their own strategic decisions. This was to have important consequences in the Peninsula, particularly after January 1809, when Napoleon left Spain and attempted to direct the war from Paris. His failure to appreciate the difficulties of campaigning in the rugged terrain of Spain and Portugal, coupled with the resilience of his opponents and the local resentment against the occupying forces, was to prove costly to his armies in the Peninsular War.

Wellesley, although the youngest lieutenant general in the British army, was already a vastly experienced commander in his own right by the time he was posted to Portugal. Born in Dublin in 1769, the fifth son of the Anglo-Irish Earl of Mornington, he joined the

British Army as an ensign in 1787 after a relatively undistinguished education at Eton, in the Netherlands, and – ironically – at a French military school. He served in several regiments and was made a captain in 1791, meanwhile gaining political experience as a member of the Irish Parliament. With money lent him by one of his older brothers, in 1793 he purchased a commission as a major in the 33rd (1st Yorkshire West Riding) Regiment of Foot, and later that same year he was promoted to lieutenant colonel and the command of his regiment while still aged only twenty-four. The purchase system – by which regimental officers bought (and sold) their ranks in the army – may have had its flaws, discriminating against able but impecunious junior officers in favour of moneyed mediocrities, but it did allow men like Wellesley to rise rapidly to the top. In 1794–5 he commanded a brigade in the 'Grand Old Duke of York's' Anglo-German campaign against the French in Flanders, commenting later that the experience taught him 'not what to do, but what not to do'. His regiment was then posted to India in 1797, where the British were engaged in a war with the powerful confederacy of Mahratta states, and where he was joined the following year by his brother Richard, who had been appointed governor-general. In 1799 Wellesley commanded the Indian element of a substantial Anglo-Indian force in the campaign against Tipu Sahib, the French-backed ruler of the independent state of Mysore, which culminated in the siege of Seringapatam. Appointed governor of the region after Tipu's defeat, Wellesley was then promoted major general in 1802 and was charged with defeating the Mahrattas in the

Deccan to the north. His hard-fought victory against overwhelming odds at the village of Assaye – in which over a third of his five thousand troops were killed or wounded – broke the Mahrattas' will to resist. By the end of 1803, after easy victories at Argaum and Gawilghur, the Deccan had been subdued and Wellesley's reputation as a fighting general established. His Indian experiences of campaigning in extreme conditions of terrain and climate were to prove invaluable in Portugal and Spain.

Wellesley arrived back in Britain in 1805, newly knighted and immensely wealthy, having accrued a fortune of £42,000 during his Indian campaigns. The following year he became a Member of Parliament,° and in 1807 was appointed Chief Secretary for Ireland. In the summer of that year he led a division during the British raid on Copenhagen, following the government's decision to interpret Danish hesitancy about whether to support Britain or France as a pretext for hostility. With the crushing of British hopes in South America, the government seized the opportunity provided by the May 1808 uprising of the Spanish against their French occupiers to despatch Wellesley to the Peninsula in order to strike a blow directly at Napoleon's forces in Europe.

Wellesley's strategy in Portugal, however, was initially defensive. Vastly outnumbered by the French, he nevertheless rapidly achieved victories at Roliça and Vimeiro, but was thwarted from fully exploiting his success when the governor of Gibraltar, Lieutenant General Sir Hew Dalrymple – who had been sent to assume overall command of the substantially reinforced British army – negotiated the Convention of Cintra which allowed the defeated French army to leave Portugal unharmed along with all its equipment and booty. Exonerated by the subsequent court of inquiry in London, Wellesley returned to Portugal in April 1809, now the commander-in-chief of British forces there. Within three months he had won the victory at Talavera which earned him the title of Viscount Wellington.

On the face of it, Wellington should have failed in the Peninsular War. Forced to rely for support on poorly equipped Portuguese and Spanish contingents (the latter also badly led), and pushed back to the border between Spain and Portugal following the dreadful retreat from Burgos towards the end of 1812, he seemed to be fighting a losing cause. But he did not waver, and his advance into Spain in the spring of 1813 was a masterpiece of military planning. News of Wellington's crushing victory over King Joseph Bonaparte at Vitoria on 21 June emboldened the conquered states elsewhere in France's European empire. Russia, Prussia and Austria picked up their arms once more and returned to the fray, slowly driving west towards France, which was still feeling the effects of the disastrous Moscow campaign at the end of 1812. Wellington, meanwhile, was making inroads in the south. By the end of 1813 Wellington was across the Pyrenees and had invaded France, while the Russians, Austrians and Prussians advanced inexorably in the north. Despite the military genius of the emperor's campaign in France in February 1814 – considered by many to have been his finest campaign – when his much reduced army inflicted four defeats on the advancing Prussians as they closed on Paris, popular support for his regime soon crumbled and he was

finally forced to abdicate on 6 April.

When the crowned heads of Europe arrived in Paris for the Allied victory parade in June 1814, there was only one man they wanted to see. When asked to describe his six years of campaigning in the Peninsula, Wellington summed up his achievement simply: 'I went abroad and took command of the Army, and never returned, or even quitted the field, till the nations of the Peninsula . . . were delivered from the French armies; till I had invaded France, won the battle of Toulouse; established the Army within French territory, of which I governed several departments; till the general peace was signed at Paris; and the British cavalry, sent by sea to Portugal, Spain and the south of France, marched home across France, and embarked for England.'

Astonishingly, Napoleon was not finished. From his exile on the Mediterranean island of Elba, he landed in France on 1 March 1815 with barely a thousand men. But the troops of the restored French King Louis XVIII sent to stop him instead joined his cause. While the court panicked and fled in the face of popular agitation to Brussels, Napoleon returned to Paris where he soon proclaimed himself 'protector' of the Revolution. Despite having almost three hundred thousand men that he was able to deploy against the Allied armies that had gathered on the borders of France to depose him, Napoleon himself was not the great man he once was. He was physically ill and perhaps beginning to show signs of mental instability. His last battle was to be Waterloo.

Even allowing for the critical intervention of Marshal Blücher's Prussian army, the great Allied victory at Waterloo in June 1815 owed most to Wellington: his choice of battleground, his deployment of his forces, and his personal leadership. Aloof, stern, never loved by his men, amongst whom there were sometimes rumblings of discontent, he had nevertheless gradually earned their respect. They recognised that he took great pains to ensure that they were well provisioned and that he endeavoured to protect them from dangerously open positions on the battlefield. This, combined with a rigidly enforced disciplinary regime, guaranteed their loyalty. When, at Sorauren in July 1813, the Portuguese troops had loudly acclaimed his arrival on the battlefield, the British soldiers had been quick to follow suit.

In the end, Wellington won through in the Peninsular War and at Waterloo because he had learned how to deploy his troops to the best effect. Unlike Napoleon, he trusted his commanders in the field, kept his troops provisioned by organised commissaries, and employed engineers to build and repair bridges on their line of march. His experience in India had also taught him the value of military intelligence. Reconnaissance by his 'exploring' officers and information obtained by Spanish guerrillas in the Peninsula contributed greatly to his successes. A further advantage was the superiority of the British line over the French offensive column. Only the first two ranks of a column could fire their muskets; the two-deep British infantry line, on the other hand, could deploy every one of its muskets against the French. Time and again in the Peninsula, and at Waterloo, Wellington demonstrated the superiority of his military tactics. It is no exaggeration to say that, without him, Napoleon might not have been defeated. Waterloo proved to be Wellington's final victory and his crowning glory, one which elevated him to an almost god-like status throughout Europe. Following his employment as commander-in-chief of the Allied forces occupying France, in 1818 he returned to Britain and a position in the Cabinet. His popularity was badly tarnished during his tenure as Prime Minister in 1828–30: his nickname, 'the Iron Duke', was a direct reference to the shutters he put up to protect the windows of his London home from the bricks thrown by a disgruntled populace. But his reputation as one of Britain's most distinguished statesmen of the age was soon restored. When he died in 1852, at the age of eighty-three, despite being born in Dublin, he was, in Queen Victoria's words, 'the greatest Englishman who ever lived'.

Chronology

1807

18 October	Junot crosses Spanish–French border
30 November	French troops occupy Lisbon

1808

23 March	French troops occupy Madrid
2 May	Dos de Mayo rising in Madrid
20 July	Wellesley lands at Corunna to consult with Spaniards
1 August	British troops begin landing in Mondego Bay, Portugal
15 August	Skirmish at Brilos, first clash between British and French in the Peninsula. Lieutenant Ralph Bunbury, of the 95th Rifles, is first British officer to be killed in the war.
17 August	Battle of Roliça
21 August	Battle of Vimeiro
31 August	Convention of Cintra
4 December	Madrid falls to the French
12 December	Moore begins retreat to Corunna

1809

16 January	Battle of Corunna; death of Sir John Moore
22 April	Wellesley resumes command of the army in Portugal
12 May	Crossing of the Douro and capture of Oporto
3 July	British army enters Spain
6 July	Wellesley becomes Marshal General of the Portuguese army
27–8 July	Battle of Talavera
4 September	Wellesley created Viscount Wellington of Talavera
20 October	Work begins on the Lines of Torres Vedras

1810

10 July	Ciudad Rodrigo surrenders to the French
24 July	Action on the river Coa
25 August	Almeida surrenders to the French
27 September	Battle of Busaco
8 October	Anglo-Portuguese army enters the Lines of Torres Vedras

1811

4 March	Masséna's retreat from Torres Vedras begins
5 March	Battle of Barrosa
15 March	Action at Foz d'Arouce
25 March	Cavalry action at Campo Mayor
3 April	Action at Sabugal
3–5 May	Battle of Fuentes de Oñoro
5–12 May	First siege of Badajoz
11 May	Garrison of Almeida escapes
16 May	Battle of Albuera
19 May–20 June	Second siege of Badajoz
25 September	Action at El Bodon
28 October	Hill's success at Arroyo dos Molinos

1812

8–19 January	Siege of Ciudad Rodrigo
5 February	Wellington becomes Earl
16 March–6 April	Third siege of Badajoz
6 April	Storming of Badajoz
May	Napoleon begins invasion of Russia
17 June	America declares war on Britain
22 July	Battle of Salamanca
12 August	Wellington enters Madrid
18 August	Wellington becomes Marquess
19 September–21 Oct	Siege of Burgos
22 October	Retreat from Burgos begins
19 November	Anglo-Portuguese army back in Portugal

1813

4 March	Wellington created Knight of the Garter
22 May	Wellington's new offensive begins
21 June	Battle of Vitoria. Wellington appointed Field Marshal

28 June	Siege of San Sebastian begins
25 July	Failed assault on San Sebastian
25 July	Battle of the Pyrenees begins: actions at Maya and Roncesvalles
28–30 July	Battle of Sorauren
31 August	Action at San Marcial
31 August	Successful assault on San Sebastian
7 October	Crossing of the Bidassoa: Wellington invades France
10 November	Battle of the Nivelle
9 December	Crossing of the Nive
10–12 December	Battle of the Nive
13 December	Battle of St Pierre

1814

15 February	Action at Garris
24 February	Crossing of the Adour
27 February	Battle of Orthes
2 March	Action at Aire
20 March	Action at Tarbes
31 March	Allies enter Paris
6 April	Napoleon abdicates
10 April	Battle of Toulouse
14 April	Sortie from Bayonne
18 April	Armistice signed. Peninsular War ends
24 April	Louis XVIII returns to France
28 April	Napoleon exiled to Elba
3 May	Wellington created Duke

Arthur Wellesley, 1st Duke of Wellington,
1769-1852. The dominant figure of the
Peninsular War.

t can be argued that the Peninsular War exploded into life n 2 May 1808 when the Madrid mob turned upon those rench troops who were attempting to carry off to France Don Francisco, the youngest son of King Carlos IV and Queen Maria Luisa of Spain. It can also be argued that it egan on 9 May, in Oviedo, the capital of the province of he Asturias, when the people came out in open revolt, eclaring war on Napoleon Bonaparte some two weeks later. n truth, the war began on 18 October 1807 when General ndoche Junot, at the head of 25,000 troops of the Army f the Gironde, crossed the Bidassoa river and set foot on panish soil in order to begin his long march to the ortuguese capital of Lisbon. By a strange irony, it was to e that very same month, six years on, that Arthur Wellesley, Marquess of Wellington, crossed the very same river to vade France and begin his final drive to victory in the eninsula, a victory which would help bring about the first ownfall of Napoleon Bonaparte in April 1814.

Portugal had long been due for Napoleon's ttention for when he stepped from his boat out onto the anks of the river Niemen after concluding the Treaty of ilsit with the Russian czar and Frederick William III of russia in July 1807, he did so having decreed that both

forced to do so. This system effectively banned all European countries from trading with Britain, France's last remaining enemy, in the vain hope that he would be able to starve her into submission. The Portuguese Regent, John, somewhat timidly bowed to pressure from both France and her ally, Spain, and declared her ports closed to British shipping. He was not, however, prepared to order the incarceration of all British citizens resident in his country and the seizure of their property. Unfortunately for the Regent, this was not good enough to satisfy Napoleon's demands and the response was Junot's advance into Spain, through which he would have to march in order to reach Lisbon.

Junot's forced march to Lisbon is one of the great dramatic episodes of the war. At the head of his 25,000 troops he set off at a rather leisurely pace on 18 October 1807 and just over three weeks later had reached Salamanca, a distance of three hundred miles. The normal route would take him on through Ciudad Rodrigo and into Portugal, past Almeida, down to Coimbra and south to Lisbon. It was the usual invasion route for armies entering Portugal and, indeed, it was the route by which Massena pursued Wellington in the late summer of 1810. However, anxious that Junot reached Lisbon before

Ciudad Rodrigo redirected him south to Alcantara and the Tagus valley. From here he was to march to Abrantes before turning south-west to Lisbon. As anyone who has ever travelled the route between Ciudad Rodrigo and Alcantara will know it is a bleak, barren wilderness of rugged but often very spectacular scenery. In his efforts to get to Lisbon Junot's men became strung out, there was little or no supplies forthcoming and when he reached Lisbon on 30 November he did so at the head of just 1,500 exhausted, tattered and rain-soaked soldiers. To add insult to injury, Junot discovered that the Portuguese Royal family had sailed for Brazil the day before. It was very fortunate that the Portuguese offered no resistance at all, otherwise Junot would have found himself on a decidedly sticky wicket. However, Portugal was taken, or at least Lisbon was, and Junot quickly set about disbanding the Portuguese army whilst trying to stamp his own authority on the city. The British ambassador, meanwhile, took ship aboard the Hibernia, the flagship of Sir Sydney Smith, whose naval

squadron arrived to begin blockading the mouth of the Tagus.

There is little need to go into the politics which were brewing up behind the scenes whilst Junot's men marched south across Spain. Suffice to say that events in Spain had been simmering away for some time before they finally came to the boil in that late autumn of 1807. Spain was, in theory, ruled by the inane King Carlos IV and his shameless, immoral wife, Queen Maria Luisa, of whom Sir Charles Oman, the great historian of the Peninsular War wrote, 'was about the most unfit person in Europe to be placed upon the throne at the side of such an imbecile husband.' In reality this hapless pair were dominated by the corrupt Manuel Godoy, the so-called 'Prince of Peace'. He had long since been their favourite and had risen to power as much by his manipulations in the corridors of power as by his many amorous nights in the Spanish Queen's bedchamber. Some acrimonious squabbling between the king and queen and Godoy, on one side, and the king's son, Ferdinand, Prince of the Asturias, on the other

The Vimeiro Battlefield Memorial.

The old road to Torres Vedras ran through this gully, up which
Wellesley's men attacked at Roliça on 17 August 1808.

The last resting place of Colonel George
Lake of the 29th, killed at Roliça.

Commemorative plaque at Vimeiro made of traditional blue Portuguese tiles.

The beach at Porto Novo, where British reinforcements came ashore on the eve of Vimeiro.

led eventually, in April 1808, to all of them being summoned by Napoleon to Bayonne where he proposed to discuss the matter of the Spanish throne. After all, both parties had sought his backing during their recent arguments which had seen, amongst other things, Ferdinand's imprisonment for treachery and Carlos' abdication in favour of his pardoned son. The shadow of the French emperor, in fact, had long been cast over affairs at the Escurial and he watched delighted as the internal strife within the Royal Family opened the way for his invasion of the country which had undoubtedly been his objective all along. Indeed, as early as January 1808 French troops began to cross the Pyrenees and the Spanish Court watched and waited with a sense of unease as column after

long column of French troops snaked over the Pyrenees into northern Spain ostensibly to march in support of Junot. By the beginning of March the important fortresses of Pamplona, San Sebastian, Barcelona and Figueras were in French hands after what Oman called 'cynical effrontery and mean cunning'.

These despicable events were followed by a further act of treachery by Napoleon at Bayonne when he declared his intention to dissolve the Bourbon family and install a French prince on the Spanish throne. By 10 May 1808, both Carlos and Ferdinand had duly signed away their rights to the Spanish throne in favour of Napoleon and Ferdinand was to spend the next six years in the chateau of Valençay under the watchful eye of his keeper, Talleyrand.

With the political antics over with, it became a simple fight for survival for the Spanish people and, as we have seen, outbreaks of violence against the French took place in Madrid on 2 May, the famous 'Dos de Mayo', which was ruthlessly suppressed by Murat, commanding the French troops in Madrid. There followed the rising already mentioned in the Asturias as well as a series of brutal sackings of Spanish towns by the invading French armies, Zaragossa held on bravely in the north whilst Andalucía felt the force of Dupont's troops as they pushed south.

The initial clashes between the French and Spanish armies went much the way of the French including their crushing victory at Medina del Rio Seco on 14 July 1808. But the really significant event took place some five days later when some 20,000 French troops, under Dupont, hemmed in along the Guadalquivir between Andujar and Baylen, surrendered to the Spaniards under Castaños. It was the first time one of Bonaparte's armies had surrendered and was the catalyst which was to bring Britain into the war on the side of the Iberian nations.

Spanish emissaries from the Asturias had arrived in London on 7 June and had sought assistance from Canning, the Foreign Secretary, who promised them arms, ammunition and money. Before the end of the month other representatives from other insurgent juntas arrived on similar missions. But it was to be Dupont's surrender at Baylen that convinced the British government that the time had finally come for a strike against Napoleon on mainland Europe and preparations were soon made for a British army to be despatched to the Iberian Peninsula as soon as possible.

The British force selected for the task consisted of some 9,000 troops who were originally destined to sail to South America in an attempt to resurrect British designs on that continent, designs which disappeared into oblivion following Whitelocke's disastrous attack on Buenos Aires in July 1807. The projected plan was abandoned, fortunately, and the force ordered to proceed to the Peninsula under the command of Sir Arthur Wellesley, the Under Secretary for Ireland. Wellesley, destined to become the dominant figure of the war, sailed to Spain and then to Portugal, where he landed on 1 August, to be joined four days later, by 5,000 men under Sir Brent Spencer. But even as Wellesley's men were tossed ashore by the rolling Atlantic waves, Sir Arthur received a despatch from Castlereagh informing him that he was to be superseded by Sir Hew Dalrymple and Sir Harry Burrard whilst another gifted soldier was likewise on his way to the Peninsula to supersede him. It was Sir John Moore.

Wellesley took this somewhat depressing news philosophically and decided that as the other generals would not arrive for a few days yet he may as well make the most of his opportunity and try to achieve as much as he could whilst he still commanded the army. His march south took him to Brilos and it was here, on 15 August 1808, that a rifleman of the 95th Rifles fired the first shot of the British campaign in the Peninsula. It was also during this skirmish that Lieutenant Ralph Bunbury, also of the 95th Rifles, achieved the somewhat unwanted distinction of becoming the first British officer to be killed in the war. Two days later, at Roliça, Wellesley's army fought its first battle of the war, a skirmish by later standards, when

Following pages, two views of the battlefield of Vimeiro. *Page 20*, a view from Wellesley's ridge, and *page 21*, a French view of the British position at Vimeiro.

The bridge over the Esla at Benavente, or Castrogonzalo as it is often called. Moore's army crossed the bridge in December 1808 before blowing it up.

Wellesley drove Delaborde from his position north of the village and then from the heights to the south of the village of Columbeira.

Four days later Wellesley achieved an even greater victory, at Vimeiro. It was here, on the slopes in front of the village, that the French columns first experienced the power of the British infantry line that sent the French reeling back in defeat. It also saw the first of a series of unhappy cavalry charges, on this occasion the culprits being the 20th Light Dragoons, with the regiment's commanding officer being killed into the bargain. The victory made more than a few heads sit up in the halls of the mighty throughout Europe and, indeed, was the beginning of a series of great victories which would take Wellesley from Lisbon to Toulouse. However, his satisfaction was soon tempered by the arrival, first of Burrard and then Dalrymple, both of whom seemed unable to act in consolidation of Wellesley's victory. The two elderly generals appeared to be paralysed and Wellesley could do nothing else but kick his heels in

frustration as the beaten French army was allowed to extricate itself unmolested.

However, Andoche Junot, commanding the French, was no fool and he realised the perilous position in which he now found himself, trapped as he was on the Lisbon peninsula. There was little choice but to ask for an armistice. Otherwise he faced the choice of a retreat back into Spain and a long and dangerous march to Burgos, where the nearest French troops were to be found, across territory infested with guerrillas who would, no doubt, reduce his army to a mere skeleton should he decide to risk this course of action. No, it was too dire to contemplate, and so General Kellerman was duly despatched to solicit terms from the British. The result was the infamous Convention of Cintra, whereby the French army was allowed to sail away in British ships, with their arms and much of their accumulated plunder, back to the safety of France. Portugal was cleared of the hated invaders at the stroke of a pen without the loss of a

Even today, the mountain roads to Corunna regularly fill with snow, as this picture, taken in January 2009, shows.

single life and without the need for prolonged sieges. After all, the fortresses of Elvas, Almeida and Peniche all had strong garrisons, protected by strong walls. The pen, on this occasion, certainly did prove mightier than the sword but the stunned British public did not see it the same way. An enemy army was there to be crushed and defeated, not to be tamely shipped home in British ships. Public anger and outrage was so widespread, in fact, that an inquiry was set up and both Dalrymple and Burrard were recalled to explain themselves, a disillusioned Wellesley already having returned home on leave. The findings of the Court found no fault with Wellesley, who was acquitted of any wrong doing. Burrard and Dalrymple, on the other hand, whilst avoiding any severe censure, never returned to the Peninsula and, indeed, faded into the backwaters of British military history.

With all three of the British generals back in England, command of the British army in Portugal devolved upon Sir John Moore, a great and experienced soldier whose methods of training light infantry remain perhaps his greatest legacy. Moore had arrived in Portugal shortly after Dalrymple but had declined to become involved with the business at Cintra. Reinforcements had increased the size of his army to 30,000 infantry with a further 15,000 expected to arrive in northern Spain in October 1808 under Sir David Baird. Moore planned to leave 10,000 troops in Lisbon whilst he himself, with the main body of the army, marched north into Spain to join up with Baird. From here, he would march to Burgos and form a junction with the Spanish generals, but he had no idea of just who he was to co-operate with.

Moore began his advance from Lisbon on 26 October 1808, his force being split into four columns, the most southerly of which saw artillery and cavalry travelling via Badajoz and Talavera to Salamanca, which was the chosen place of concentration. The army began to concentrate towards mid-November but while he waited at Salamanca, he received unwanted information that the Spaniards had

been scattered to the winds by Napoleon – who had ventured south of the Pyrenees in person with the intention of sweeping the British into the sea – and that there was little prospect of co-operating with them. Consequently, Moore issued orders for a retreat towards Corunna and Vigo, while the British reinforcements under Baird, which had finally landed during the first week of November, were ordered to turn about and march back the way they had come. However, on 4 December Hope's column finally staggered into Salamanca to find that Moore had changed his mind and had decided to advance instead. This was based upon assurances given to him by the Spaniards who claimed they were about to begin a defence of Madrid. Moore decided that he would march north to Burgos after all and threaten Napoleon's communications with France. By doing so he hoped to draw the French away from Madrid and afford the defenders some time to organise themselves. Little did he know, however, that by the time his advance began, on 11 December, Madrid had been in the hands of the French invaders for a whole week, having fallen on 4 December, the very day that Hope's column arrived at Salamanca.

One of the great characteristics of the Corunna campaign was the way in which both sides groped around in almost complete ignorance of the exact whereabouts of each other. This lack of reliable intelligence was highlighted on 23 December when Moore received an intercepted despatch that told him the bad news that Madrid had fallen. This, however, was accompanied by useful information that Soult was isolated with a fairly weak force in his front, upon which Moore decided to attack him. The optimism with which Moore's army began its march was cruelly shattered by the news that Napoleon was leading his imperial legions over the snows of the Guadarrama Pass in order to drive 'the hideous leopard' into the sea. British hopes were dashed, as were hundreds of British muskets as Moore's men threw them to the ground in utter frustration. The retreat to Corunna had begun.

Events in Galicia were, therefore, turning sour for the British. And, even as they contemplated the thought of a gruelling retreat, their Spanish Allies were reeling from one defeat after another as the French began to push out into Spain. The Spanish armies had already been defeated at Medina, as we have seen, and by the end of the year they would experience further disasters at Gamonal, Espinosa, Cardadeu and at Molins del Rey. And yet the Spaniards themselves were to make a major contribution to the war in Spain merely by their presence and would prevent the French from turning their full attention to the relatively small British – and later Anglo-Portuguese – army. When the war was over Wellington paid a great tribute to the Spanish guerrillas, even suggesting that without their contribution he could not have driven the French from the Peninsula. But we must never overlook the role of the Spanish armies themselves, who doggedly and bravely maintained a threatening presence in the field in spite of a succession of defeats. In fact, the Spaniards would come to regard the role of the British army as being a fairly minor one, given the fact that until 1813 all that the Spanish people ever seemed to see of their British allies was during a retreat – 1809, 1810, 1811 and even 1812 saw the British conducting retreats back to Portugal. Indeed, it is interesting to note the

Left, A stretch of the Galician hills through which Moore's army passed during the retreat to Corunna in 1808-09.

Following page, top, the bridge at Constantino, scene of Paget's rearguard fight in January 1809, and *below*, the bridge at Nogales.

The Burial of Sir John Moore After Corunna
Charles Wolfe, 1791-1823

Not a drum was heard, not a funeral note,
As his corse to the rampart we hurried;
Not a soldier discharged his farewell shot
O'er the grave where our hero we buried.

We buried him darkly at dead of night,
The sods with our bayonets turning;
By the struggling moonbeam's misty light
And the lanthorn dimly burning.

No useless coffin enclosed his breast,
Not in sheet or in shroud we wound him;
But he lay like a warrior taking his rest
With his martial cloak around him.

Few and short were the prayers we said,
And we spoke not a word of sorrow;
But we steadfastly gazed on the face that was dead,
And we bitterly thought of the morrow.

We thought, as we hollow'd his narrow bed
And smooth'd down his lonely pillow,
That the foe and the stranger would tread o'er his head,
And we far away on the billow!

Lightly they'll talk of the spirit that's gone
And o'er his cold ashes upbraid him –
But little he'll reck, if they let him sleep on
In the grave where a Briton has laid him.

But half of our heavy task was done
When the clock struck the hour for retiring:
And we heard the distant and random gun
That the foe was sullenly firing.

Slowly and sadly we laid him down,
From the field of his fame fresh and gory;
We carved not a line, and we raised not a stone,
But we left him alone with his glory.

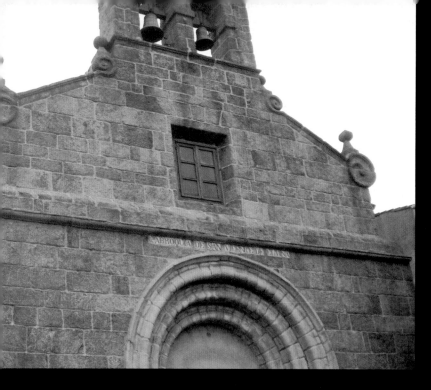

EN ESTA CASA
MURIÓ EL VALEROSO GENERAL INGLÉS
SIR. JOHN MOORE
EL 16 DE ENERO DE 1809,
Á CONSECUENCIA DE LAS HERIDAS
QUE RECIBIÓ EL MISMO DÍA
EN LA BATALLA DE ELVIÑA
LUCHANDO HEROICAMENTE EN DEFENSA
DE LA INDEPENDENCIA ESPAÑOLA.
PRIMER CENTENARIO.
1909

amount of fighting done between 1808 and 1814 by both the Spanish and Anglo-Portuguese armies. A relatively crude but nevertheless useful exercise is to compare the number of trophies captured during the war by the two Allied armies. The Spanish armies captured some eleven eagles and thirty-one flags from their French opponents compared to just six eagles and sixteen flags captured by the Anglo-Portuguese. This, admittedly, is a simple exercise but it does give some indication to the amount of fighting done by the Spanish armies, something which is very often overlooked by historians today who tend to focus on the role of the guerrillas.

On 16 January 1809, Sir John Moore and his savage, tattered and exhausted army turned in anger on their French tormentors who had hustled and harried them through the snow-covered mountains of Galicia. They demonstrated that in spite of the often terrible conditions endured by them during the horrors of the retreat, they were still capable of fighting and, indeed, delivered a loud

message to the French, that a British soldier is never more at his dangerous and magnificent best than when his back is firmly against the wall. At the battle of Corunna, the British army turned and fought off successive French attacks to enable itself to embark aboard the ships of the Royal Navy, waiting anxiously in the harbour. Sadly, Sir John Moore was not amongst them, for as his men shuffled onto the ships he lay dying in a house in the Canton Grande of a terrible wound to the chest and shoulder. As the first ships began to sail away towards England Moore was lowered into his grave and there, on the ramparts of the Old Town, he was, in the words of the poem, left alone with his glory.

While Moore had been busy in Spain Wellesley was back in England, defending himself against the various charges which had arisen following the Convention of Cintra. Fortunately, he was acquitted and by April 1809 he was back in command of the British army in Portugal. The task facing him was not an enviable one and his arrival in Portugal came

Opposite, clockwise, plaque marking the house where Moore died, French view of Elvina on the Corunna battlefield, tile map of the battle, and the church at Elvina.

The modern battlefield memorial at Talavera.

on the back of another succession of Spanish defeats at Valls, Ciudad Real and the Medellin. The city of Zaragoza had also fallen after a brave and heroic defence by the population and their commander, Palafox. Over 54,000 inhabitants died during the two-month siege during which the French fought their way into the city, house by house, in savage and bitter fighting.

Within just three weeks of landing Wellesley had formulated his plan for the forthcoming campaign, to drive Soult from Portugal before marching south into Spain to link up with the Spaniards against Victor. The crossing of the Douro at Oporto was one of Wellesley's most daring operations, involving small groups of British infantry who crossed the river in wine barges while the French defenders peered aimlessly out to the west and to the sea, from which direction they expected the British attack to come. By the time Soult realised just what was going on Wellesley's men had fortified the Bishop's Seminary, a large building to the east of the town, whilst Sherbrooke's brigade had crossed the

river from the suburb of Villa Nova de Gaia. The operation was a complete success and so ended the second French invasion of Portugal. Wellesley was back and he was not to leave the Peninsula until the war was finally over in 1814.

Wellesley's return had been a great success and, for a general who has long since been regarded as a defensive-minded commander, the crossing of the Douro was all the more significant. However, the operation did not herald the beginning of a period of British success in the Peninsula. When Wellesley marched into Spain to meet his Spanish allies he must have done so with some degree of trepidation, given the absence of co-operation showed towards Moore during the latter's ill-fated Corunna campaign. He was not to be disappointed. He met the ageing General Cuesta in a small village close to Almaraz and even by the dim light of the burning torches by which he inspected Cuesta's men he could see that he was going to have his work cut out if he was to forge a working relationship with them. The Spaniards

Previous pages, Porto. *Page 30*, a view of Sherbrooke's crossing point over the Douro from the Serra do Pilar. *Page 31*, another view of the same, this time from the level of the river outside the port lodges of Vila Nova de Gaia.

regarded the British as heretics whilst they themselves were loathe to do today what they could put off until tomorrow. They were also very proud men and could not bring themselves to accept orders from their British allies. As it turned out, their first major battle together, at Talavera on 27-28 July 1809, ended in victory for them, although the brunt of the fighting fell fairly and squarely on the red-jacketed soldiers whose firepower and steady lines proved too much for Victor's French columns. It was a costly victory for Wellesley – some 5,365 British soldiers were killed or wounded – but it was one which earned for him the title 'Wellington'.

The Battle of Talavera had ushered in a period of fourteen months of great tension and anxiety for Wellington and his army as they watched and waited in the north upon the Portuguese-Spanish border for Marshal André Massena to begin what would be the third French invasion of Portugal. Elsewhere, however, the war went on, with the Spaniards winning at Tamames on 18 October 1809, their first victory since Alcaniz on 23

May that year. This victory, however, was more scant reward for a year of hard endeavour which had seen their armies beaten yet again at Almonacid, Ocaña and Alba de Tormes, and the city of Gerona fall after yet another violent siege. It was this fourteen-month period that saw the emergence of the so-called 'croakers', British officers, several of high rank, who advocated an abandonment of the campaign in the Peninsula and who conspired ineffectively but irritatingly against Wellington. The commander-in-chief was not to be put off by the croakers but their whisperings and whinges were a constant source of annoyance to him. The views of the croakers also found voice amongst politicians at home who saw little point in remaining in the Peninsula and, indeed, when Ciudad Rodrigo and Almeida fell to Massena in the summer of 1810 Wellington's position looked very precarious. However, unbeknown to all but a few of his closest confidants, Wellington had been planning ahead for such an eventuality. Indeed, on 26 October 1809, Wellington had given orders for

Fort Conception, blown up before being abandoned by the British in July 1810.

the construction of a series of defensive lines to be laid out across the Lisbon peninsula from the Atlantic to the Tagus. These were the famous Lines of Torres Vedras, since dubbed 'the cheapest investment in military history' and certainly one of the best kept secrets in history. Wellington, with unerring accuracy, predicted that the French invasion would be too strong to hold back on the border itself and that his army would have to

retreat to the relative security of the lines, by which time much of the Portuguese population north of Lisbon would have been driven inside the lines along with their livestock and crops, leaving the land to be laid waste behind them. He even predicted that he would turn and make a stand along the way, which he did at Busaco. It all fell out as he expected.

Throughout the spring and summer of 1810 Wellington's army

waited on the Portuguese border as Massena's preparations for the French invasion pressed on. There were numerous skirmishes on both the Coa and Agueda rivers as the newly-formed Light Division, under the command of its controversial leader, Robert 'Black Bob' Craufurd, strove mightily to prevent the ever probing French from piercing Wellington's outpost line in order to gain information on Allied troop dispositions. Much of the reputation of the Light Division as being Wellington's élite division was gained during this period, and not once did it let its commander down. The chain of outposts along the Coa and Agueda was such that, as Sir Charles Oman later wrote, 'the whole web of communication quivered at the slightest touch.' Indeed, the seeds sewn by Sir John Moore during his famous period of training of the light infantry at Shorncliffe can be said to have come to fruition on the rocky chasms of the river Coa. But while the Light Division enjoyed a period of prolonged and active service at the outposts, the rest of the Allied army wallowed in frustration and idleness which gave more weight to the arguments of the

Previous pages, Talavera. *Page 34*, a view from the northern slope of the Medellin, looking into the valley where the 23rd Light Dragoons came to grief. The area is now covered by a reservoir. *Page 35*, The Pajar de Vagara, a fortified position on the battlefield, as seen from the British lines.

croakers who now, more than ever, saw little point in remaining in the Peninsula, particularly with the prospect of a French invasion in strength looming on the horizon. Many officers grew jealous of the Light Division and its escapades and as one of its officers later recalled, the mere mention of the words 'outposts' or 'Light Division' was enough to turn many officers' wine ration into vinegar! That the Light Division performed sterling work on the border there can be little doubt, but there were more than the occasional bad episode which sent Wellington into the depths of frustration, none more so than at Barquilla, on 11 July 1810, and, more particularly, during the infamous combat of the Coa, on 24 July. During this latter action part of Ney's VI Corps attacked Craufurd as he prepared to bring his division back over to the left bank of the Coa river. Attacked in strength, Craufurd was driven back pell-mell on the Coa, across which there lay just a single bridge which quickly became the scene of much confusion and chaos as the British and Portuguese infantry came tumbling down the hillsides to cross. That the

A view of the Tagus from Fort 41, the Lines of Torres Vedras

Light Division managed to escape at all was down purely to the skill of the division's battalion commanders, for all control at higher level was lost almost immediately. Three hundred and ninety-two casualties was the price for Craufurd's folly in delaying far longer than he ought to have done whilst the French also suffered heavily, mainly in their attempts to pass the bridge after Craufurd's men had finally crossed it. Craufurd's reputation was dented even

if Wellington wrote that his mistake was one of judgement rather than intention. It could have been far worse however, for the loss of the Light Division may have given the croakers more ammunition than even Wellington himself could have sustained. It is just as well that elsewhere in the Iberian Peninsula French efforts were concentrated mainly in Catalonia, Valencia and Andalucía as they fought hard to

Left, the Great Redoubt at Sobral at the time of renovations in 2008. *Below*, the Torres Vedras memorial to Sir Richard Fletcher at Alhandra.

consolidate their stranglehold on the country.

By the end of August 1810, both Ciudad Rodrigo and Almeida were in Massena's hands, the latter most fortuitously after one of the first shots fired by his guns ignited a leaky powder keg which train led back to the main magazine. In the ensuing terrible explosion over 500 Portuguese were killed. Also, the extra time which Wellington had hoped a prolonged defence of Almeida would buy him was now spent and his army was forced to withdraw into Portugal a little more hurriedly than was originally planned. While the army trudged west the construction of the Lines of Torres Vedras, or Lines of Lisbon as they were originally called, gathered apace. Royal Engineer officers were despatched to Lisbon to report on their progress. Some of the officers suggested the lines would not hold back the French for five minutes and that the Portuguese would run at the first shots. However, things were to turn out quite different. For the moment there was still the matter of a delaying action, which Wellington had

predicted, and it finally came on 27 September 1810 with the Battle of Busaco.

The morning of the 27th dawned grey and misty and found the Allied army settled in atop a ridge which towered some eighteen hundred feet above sea level and extended for over eleven miles north from the Mondego. That the French even considered a frontal attack on this position is testament to both their confidence and ability but these qualities alone would not be enough to dislodge the Allied defenders and a series of attacks by Massena's columns were driven back after some fearsome hard fighting, leaving Wellington in possession of the ridge. However, some miles to the north Massena's troops discovered a route by which they were able to outflank Wellington's left flank and once again the Allied army was chivvied along towards Lisbon.

Eventually, on 10 October 1810, Wellington's army entered the lines with Massena close behind. It was a bewildered Massena, too, for he gazed up in total astonishment at the defences, the existence of which he was

Previous pages, Page 38, a view of the gorge of the Agueda river at Barba del Puerco, and the Roman bridge crossing it. *Page 39*, the superbly constructed Fort Concepcion at Aldea del Obispo. Built in 1730, it was blown up by the retiring British in July 1810.

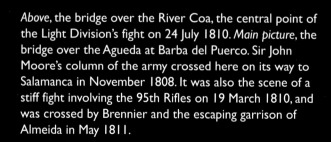

Above, the bridge over the River Coa, the central point of the Light Division's fight on 24 July 1810. *Main picture*, the bridge over the Agueda at Barba del Puerco. Sir John Moore's column of the army crossed here on its way to Salamanca in November 1808. It was also the scene of a stiff fight involving the 95th Rifles on 19 March 1810, and was crossed by Brennier and the escaping garrison of Almeida in May 1811.

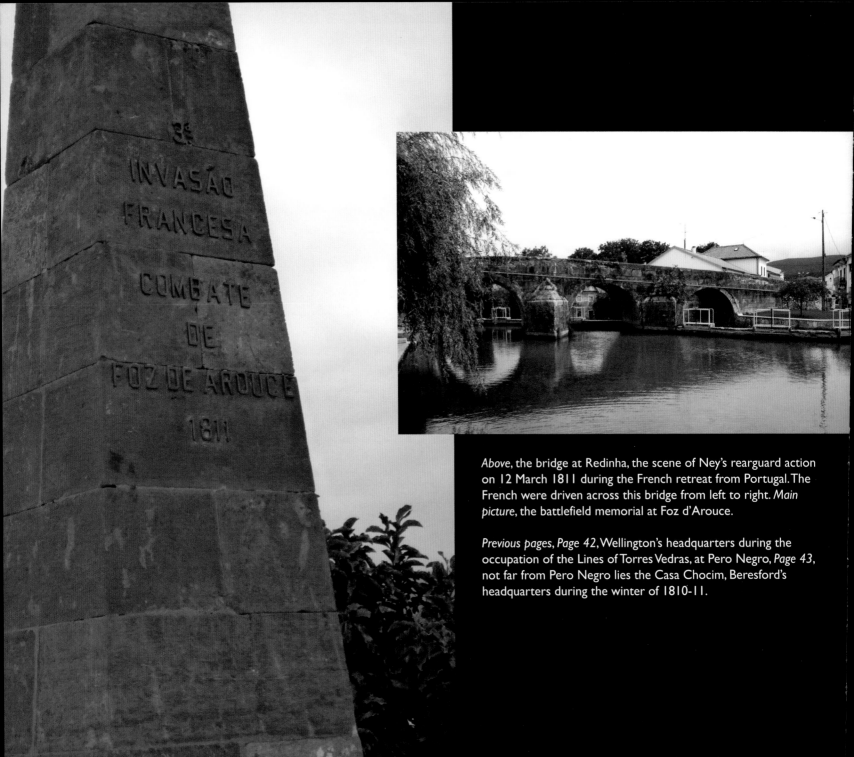

Above, the bridge at Redinha, the scene of Ney's rearguard action on 12 March 1811 during the French retreat from Portugal. The French were driven across this bridge from left to right. *Main picture*, the battlefield memorial at Foz d'Arouce.

Previous pages, Page 42, Wellington's headquarters during the occupation of the Lines of Torres Vedras, at Pero Negro, *Page 43*, not far from Pero Negro lies the Casa Chocim, Beresford's headquarters during the winter of 1810-11.

Foz d'Arouce, scene of the French rearguard action on 15 March 1811, as seen from the French defensive line.

completely unaware. In fact, the concept of the lines had been known only to a very few select officers close to Wellington. True, many people knew all about the construction of various forts and redoubts but few appear to have appreciated the way in which they linked together to form what was to prove an impenetrable barrier to Massena who only once, at Sobral on 14 October, tested them in any great strength and with little

success. Massena lingered before the lines for three weeks before deciding to pull back to Santarem, a few miles to the north, where provisions could be obtained, the land occupied by his troops in front of the lines having been stripped bare. Once more the French settled down to wait and watch but for what? There was no chance of help forthcoming from far off Paris whilst Wellington himself showed very little inclination to move out from the safety

of the lines, fed and supplied as he was by the ships of the Royal Navy. The situation dragged on until 5 March 1811 when the British piquets moved forward to discover that the very stiff French sentries in front of them were, in fact, simply dummies stuffed with straw. Massena was finally in full retreat.

The French retreat through Portugal was marked by an outburst of savagery as village after village was laid waste, and put to the torch. Indeed, the roads taken by Massena's army were strewn with the corpses of murdered men, women and children, many of whom had been tortured first. Wellington's men were horrified by what they discovered. The French themselves did not escape punishment and any stragglers who strayed too far from the main French columns were bound to fall prey to the watching, waiting Portuguese guerrillas who were capable of evening the score in the most terrible manner.

As Massena's starving army marched north it was followed all the way by Wellington who ensured that the pressure was kept on all the way back to Spain. There were fights at Redinha, Pombal, Cazal Nova, Foz d'Arouce – where the French lost one of their prized Imperial 'eagles' – and finally at Sabugal, before Massena was finally thrown back over the border and into Spain. The third and final French invasion had come to a disastrous end. So decisive did the Lines of Torres Vedras prove, that the present Duke of Wellington was moved to write that, 'if in the course of the history of war a battle had taken place in which one side lost 30,000 men and the other a matter of a few hundreds, it would have echoed down the pages of history as the greatest victory ever won. But that, in fact, is the decisive nature of Massena's defeat at the Lines of Torres Vedras. It was possibly the most decisive victory that Wellington won during the entire Peninsular Campaign.'

Portugal was finally clear of Massena's army but there still remained holding out in the fortress of Almeida a French garrison under General Brennier and it was the operation to relieve them that led to the final confrontation in the Peninsula between Wellington and his most dogged and able adversary, Massena. The battle of Fuentes de Onoro was fought over three days, between 3 and 5 May 1811, and saw a great deal of bloodshed in the maze of small streets and alleyways of which the village consisted. Wave after wave of French infantry crossed the Dos Casas stream to do battle with Wellington's men in the streets only to be thrust back again after severe and savage hand-to-hand fighting. The battle continued with a series of assaults on the village while away to the south French pressure forced Wellington to withdraw his right flank, the squares of the Light Division covering the operation in what was later described as 'a series of rhythmical evolutions which transformed the deadly orthodoxy of Hyde Park reviews into a dance of life.' Massena's attempt to relieve the garrison of Almeida ended in failure and a few days later a messenger was on his way from Paris bearing a despatch from the Emperor recalling him to France and informing him that Marshal Auguste Marmont was to assume command in his place. Ironically, Brennier blew up the fortifications of Almeida shortly before midnight on 10 May and bravely led his garrison through the Allied blockade to safety with the loss of 360 men, an operation which an exasperated Wellington claimed had turned the victory at Fuentes de Onoro into a defeat.

With Massena now gone, the biggest threat to Wellington's progress was removed. However, in the south Marshal Soult, who had already driven Moore from Spain but who had in turn been driven from Portugal by Wellington in 1809, returned to the Peninsula to begin the conquest of Estremadura and Andalucía. His initial

Wellington's headquarters at Freneida, on the Portuguese border and close to the battlefield of Fuentes de Onoro

operations got off to an optimistic start with the capture of both Olivenza and Badajoz, coupled with the French victory at Gebora. Like other French commanders he was to find his task in Spain to be a far cry from operations in central Europe and ultimately was to fail. Soult and Marmont were just two of a series of French commanders sent to the Peninsula to deal with both the Spanish and the Anglo-Portuguese armies. In the event none of them was successful, thanks in part to interference from Paris by Napoleon himself who never really appreciated the great difficulties facing his commanders, he himself only paying a brief visit south of the Pyrenees in the winter of 1808-09. He had also underestimated the great dangers posed to his southern border by an increasingly successful Allied army. Of course, he was more often than not tied down by affairs in central Europe, in particular the ill-fated Russian campaign of 1812. But one wonders whether Napoleon made a significant error in not taking the war in the Peninsula more seriously. It appears to have been to him merely a drain on

French resources – a 'running sore' or 'ulcer' he was to call it later – but in reality it was much more than this. Indeed, not only did it provide an inroad into France from the south, taking the pressure off the often beleaguered Allied powers in the north, but it gave the British army the opportunity of honing a fine blade of what began as a blunt instrument; after all, the army went into the Peninsula campaign on the back of a very patchy war record. The victories in Egypt and India were as distant a memory as they were far off in terms of distance, whilst the disasters of El Hamet in Egypt in 1807 and Buenos Aires in the same year were still fresh in the memory. Only the small but very significant victory of Sir John Stuart's army at Maida could be held up with any satisfaction at the outset of the war. Therefore, the long years of war in the green valleys of Portugal, on the dusty plains of Leon and atop the high, rugged mountains of the Pyrenees gave Wellington's men the opportunity to graduate from a small and very delicate army into what Wellington described in November 1813 as 'the most

1811 - 2006
HOMENAGEM
A TODOS QUANTOS PERECERAM
NO COMBATE DA REDINHA

complete machine for its numbers now existing in Europe'. It was a chance grabbed eagerly by Wellington's men and they were not to let their commander down.

Of course, in 1811 the British army had a long way to go before it was in a position to earn such high praise from Wellington as that which he accorded it in 1813. But it had seen off Massena and for that Wellington could be thankful, as he had proved his most dogged enemy. Marmont was a different case altogether and his term of office would last barely fourteen months. Meanwhile, the main theatre of operations shifted to the south, to Estremadura and Andalucía. In May and June 1811, the Allied army laid siege to the fortress of Badajoz, but with little success. Indeed, the siege operations served to demonstrate that Wellington's engineers were simply not up to the job and that it would take a very real effort to snatch the place from the grasp of the French. How true this was to prove in April 1812. The siege operations at Badajoz were interrupted by the battle of Albuera, fought on 16 May 1811, between Beresford and

Soult. It was the bloodiest battle of th war in terms of sheer pummelling. Th Allied victory was purchased at terrible cost to the British infantr however, who stood there pouring ou volley after volley, into the packe ranks of Frenchmen who gave as goo as they got until they could take n more. 'Survivors who took part did s as in a dream,' the great historian of th British army later wrote, 'with a littl inclining to the centre but above all desire not to run.' And he was right But one wonders whether the drean was really a nightmare, for it surel must have been for those brave men or both sides who stood opposite eac other, firing blindly through the smok in the dark ranks opposite them 'Bloody Albuera' was the mos controversial battle of the war, owin to the bad position adopted b Beresford and by his efforts to redeen the position which he should hav taken up in the first place. Only th steadfastness of the stoic Britis infantrymen saved him that day Indeed, Soult later said that the da was his but that the British did no know it and would not run.

Two great battles, fought within days of each other in May 1811. *Opposite*, two views of the main fighting area at Albuera. British and French infantry fought to the death on these slopes, *top*, whilst, *bottom*, the 3rd (Buffs) were slaughtered by French and Polish cavalry on this knoll. *This page, main picture*, the fields outside Poco Velho, the starting point for Craufurd's great retirement during the Battle of Fuentes de Onoro. *Right*, alleyways of death. A typical alley in the small village of Fuentes de Onoro, where the savage hand-to-hand fighting was at its worst.

A view of part of the battlefield of Fuentes de Onoro, looking north towards Poco Velho from the fields just north of Nave de Haver. Cotton's cavalry fought Montbrun's cavalry across these fields in the right distance on what was described by Fortescue as one of the greatest days in the history of British cavalry.

But it was not all bad news in 1811. Indeed, at Barrosa, on 5 March, Sir Thomas Graham led his men up the hill there to defeat Marshal Victor and his army in a fierce battle, during which the 87th's Sergeant Patrick Masterson took the Imperial 'eagle' of the French 8th Line Regiment. It was the first of six such trophies to be taken during the war.

Back in the north, Marmont's tenure of office began with a series of complicated, drawn-out manoeuvres on the Spanish-Portuguese border, culminating in a stand-off as the year came to a close. Winter arrived and the campaigning season duly came to an end. Or so Marmont thought. For while his men settled down for the coming winter, Wellington's men busied themselves in making preparations for their assault on Ciudad Rodrigo, the first of the great fortresses to fall to them.

The strategic importance of Ciudad Rodrigo lay in the fact that it commanded the northern corridor between Spain and Portugal. Before Wellington could even consider advancing into Spain he would have to

prise these guardians of the frontier from the French; indeed, they were not called 'the keys of Spain' for nothing. Wellington's thrust was also aided by further interference from Napoleon who ordered the withdrawal of 12,000 French troops under Dorsenne from the border in order to assist Suchet in the east, a move which gave the Allied commander far greater freedom of movement. The fateful siege of Ciudad Rodrigo began on 8 January 1812 amidst snow and biting cold winds. The frozen ground made digging almost impossible to begin with but through sheer hard work the infantry – Wellington possessed no such luxury as a corps of sappers and miners – managed to dig trenches or 'parallels' in which the guns were then placed in batteries. They sapped forward from the Greater Teson, the hill overlooking the town, and down to the Lesser Teson, a lower height just a few hundred yards from the walls of the fortress itself. By the evening of 19 January all was ready. Wellington's gunners had laid low the town walls in two places, creating two practicable breaches. Craufurd's Light Division

Previous pages, detail from two of the largest memorials in the Peninsula. *Page 56*, Oporto, and *Page 57*, Vitoria.

was to storm the Lesser Breach whilst the 3rd Division, under General Henry Mackinnon, would assault the Greater Breach. Two diversionary attacks were also to be made, one across the bridge over the Agueda against the defences below the castle and another from the convent of Santa Cruz against the left of the main breach. The attack was duly delivered by the storming columns which moved slowly forward in the darkness, feeling their way towards the breaches under fire from the French defenders. Craufurd's Light Division was first up, scrambling their way up and into the Lesser Breach meeting with relatively light resistance. In fact, so quickly was their passage into the town that, after turning to their right in order to clear the ramparts as far as the Great Breach, many of them were killed when the French exploded a huge mine beneath it. Scores of British troops from the 3rd Division were sent flying into the air along with several men of the Light Division who had been too quick for their own good and died in the explosion

Palm trees inside the alcazaba at Badajoz.

The site of the Lesser Breach, Ciudad Rodrigo, now an entrance to the town.

The ditch of Fort San Christobal, Badajoz.

The great Roman bridge over the Tagus at Alcantara.

The town was taken, but at a great cost. Both commanders of the respective storming columns were lost during the assault, Mackinnon being killed by the great mine and Craufurd being mortally wounded by a French musket ball as he stood upon the glacis, urging his beloved Light Division forward. Five hundred and sixty-two officers and men were either killed or wounded during the storming. The first of the two great fortresses was now in Wellington's hands but there was a darker and more significant aspect to the successful storming, for, in the event of such a success, nobody appears to have considered what they should do afterwards. No British army had ever taken a town by storm in the Peninsula – indeed, the British army had not taken a regularly fortified town in Europe since Drogheda back in 1649. When Wellington's men broke into Ciudad Rodrigo officers lost control of their men and there was a period of disorder during which they broke open houses and shops in search of drink and plunder. Some buildings were also set on fire. The disorder was relatively short lived and order was restored after a few hours. The most significant aspect of these disturbances, however, was that it gave Wellington's men a taste of what they could expect to enjoy at Badajoz, their next objective, for if affairs were bad at Rodrigo they would be much worse there in the maze of small, dark streets where order would be virtually impossible for British officers to maintain over any troops determined to break free from the rigours of army discipline. Furthermore, Badajoz had a long history amongst the British troops as being a distinctly hostile town and had shown itself thus during the aftermath of Talavera in 1809 when British troops – particularly the wounded – were afforded a less than friendly welcome from their supposed Spanish allies. Also, Wellington's men had besieged the town twice before, in May and June 1811, without any success, and this served only to increase their determination to settle the score when they revisited the town in April 1812. The situation cannot be summed up any better than by a passage from William Grattan, an officer of the 88th (Connaught Rangers), who wrote, 'the capture of Badajoz had long been their idol; many causes led to this wish on their part; the two previous unsuccessful sieges, and the failure of the attack against San Cristobal in the latter; but above all, the well known hostility of its inhabitants to the British army, and perhaps might be added, a desire for plunder which the sacking of Rodrigo had given them a taste for. Badajoz was, therefore, denounced as a place to be made an example of; and most unquestionably no city, Jerusalem exempted, was ever more strictly visited to the letter than was this ill-fated town.' He could not have put it better.

First of all, of course, Wellington had to move his army south, which he began to do in February 1812. A series of ruses was employed to lead the French into believing that there would be no further offensive moves for the time being. The number of sick and wounded in hospitals was exaggerated, some senior officers were allowed to go home on leave, whilst Wellington himself remained at Freneida until 5 March. Then, quickly, and without fuss, he slipped away to join his army which had appeared to the west of Badajoz. The great siege was about to begin.

The siege of Badajoz was, from the outset, a race against time with relieving French armies marching to the town's assistance. Wellington was again hampered by a lack of decent siege tools whilst the digging devolved once again on the ordinary line regiments. The weather conspired against him also, with the rain pouring down in torrents during the first days of the siege which began on 16 March. However, by sheer hard work and through the skill of Wellington's gunners, two breaches were made in the strong walls of the town – in the bastions of the Santa Maria and La Trinidad – with another being blasted on 5 April through the curtain wall which connected them. With time running out Wellington – probably with a heavy heart, for he almost certainly would have liked more time to batter the walls – issued his orders for the assault. The main storming columns were to be provided by the 4th and Light Divisions, who were to attack the breaches, whilst Picton's 3rd Division was to make a diversionary attack by escalading the high walls of the Moorish castle in the north-eastern

The year 1812 was once picked out in cannonballs, marking the site of the great breach in the Trinidad bastion at Badajoz.

quarter of the town. Leith's 5th Division was to make a second diversionary attack, on the Pardaleras fort and against the San Vicente bastion.

When the cathedral bells in Badajoz tolled the hour of ten o'clock on the night of 6 April 1812, they heralded the beginning of the most momentous, dramatic and terrible night of the whole Peninsular War. Whilst thousands of British and Portuguese troops waited to move into the attack around 5,000 determined French troops waited for them behind a series of deadly defences which blocked the breaches and barred all entrances into the town. Each defender at the breaches was armed with at least three muskets. In all, it was a veritable hell into which Wellington's attacking divisions were hurled. The 4th and Light Divisions were thrown against the walls of Badajoz no less than forty times, but in vain. Each time they were thrown back by the tenacious defenders who were commanded by Governor Armand Phillipon, as staunch an opponent as Wellington would come up against in the

Peninsula. But while the French defenders taunted and jeered their increasingly desperate attackers at the breaches, other British troops were pouring over the ramparts at the castle and at the San Vincente to render their efforts useless. Soon, British bugles could be heard faintly above the roar at the breaches and, as the defenders realised the enemy was approaching from behind them, resistance ceased and Badajoz was won. It was won at a tremendous cost, however, for no less than 3,752 British and Portuguese troops became casualties, including over 800 killed, and most of these were confined to a relatively small area at the breaches. Little wonder that Wellington broke down and wept when he saw the horrifying carnage there on the morning of 7 April.

Inside the town, meanwhile, those who had survived the assault unleashed their full power against the town and its unfortunate population. Shops and houses were sacked, their contents looted, women and young girls were raped and murdered, convents were sacked and pillaged and all manner of atrocities committed that defy description. Seventy-two hours later – an astonishing length of time for an army to be out of control – the debauchery died down. Wellington's efforts to restore order, including the erection of a gallows that, incidentally, was not used, came to nothing and, as Napier later wrote, 'the disorder subsided rather than was quelled.'

Many may claim, with some justification, that Wellington's men were entitled to embark upon their course. After all, by fighting on after practicable breaches had been made in the walls of the town – the convention current at the time dictating that garrisons should surrender in such

an event – the French waived all rights to mercy. Wellington himself later wrote that if he had slaughtered the garrison at Ciudad Rodrigo he would have saved the flower of his army at Badajoz. But he did not, the garrison at Badajoz fought on, and the consequences were left for all to see. Curiously, it was not the French garrison which suffered, but the population, leading one to suspect that the British troops were bent on such a design from the outset. As Grattan says, Badajoz was a town to be made an example of.

Wellington's army staggered away from Badajoz and returned north, ironically to avert a renewed threat to Ciudad Rodrigo by Marmont who quickly withdrew. The subsequent operations saw Wellington march east to Salamanca, which was entered on 17 June 1812. There followed a period of marching and counter-marching by both French and Allied armies before Marmont pushed his luck too far on 22 July at the small village of Los Arapiles, a few miles south of Salamanca. Here, the French extended their left too far in an attempt to cut Wellington's retreat to Portugal and as a horrified Marmont watched the disastrous manoeuvre unfold before him Wellington's divisions struck south against his columns, destroying one after another. So much, therefore, for the defensive-minded and over-cautious reputation of the British commander. The battle did not go completely in Wellington's favour, however, for after Pack and Cole had seen their attacks thwarted by some stout French resistance, the French commander, Clausel – both Marmont and his successor, Bonnet, had been struck down and carried from the field – launched a fierce counter-attack

Previous pages, Salamanca. *Page 62*, it was along this valley that Le Marchant's heavy cavalry swept to destroy almost eight battalions of French infantry. *Page 63*, A view of the central part of the battlefield looking north-east towards the Greater Arapil, with the Lesser Arapil to the left. It remains one of Europe's greatest battlefields.

which almost succeeded. Fortunately, Wellington displayed his powers of foresight again, and while Cole's men rallied Clinton's 6th Division was thrust by him into the gap to prevent the French from snatching a drawn battle, if not victory itself, from what had earlier appeared to be a disaster. As night fell, Marmont's defeated army was driven from the field in disorder and it was only the darkness, and an extensive wood to the south of the battlefield, that saved the French from a greater disaster. Wellington did not pursue the French. And why should he? For had he not despatched Carlos D'España's Spanish troops to Alba de Tormes to hold the only bridge over the Tormes river? There was no other way for the retreating French to cross the Tormes and it would be a simple matter for his army to advance the following morning and scoop them all up. Unfortunately, D'España had withdrawn his men without any orders and had understandably not the courage to inform Wellington of this wholly unauthorised movement. The commander-in-chief's reaction – he was never one to tolerate the slightest

deviation from his orders – can be easily imagined. Despite this disappointing conclusion, the battle of Salamanca was a crushing defeat for the French and was one which, in the opinion of Foy, one of the defeated French generals, raised Wellington's reputation throughout Europe to that of Marlborough.

Victory at Salamanca opened the way to Madrid which was entered by Wellington on 12 August. It was a time of great optimism for the Allies in Spain, for not only had the first eight months of the year yielded some of the great triumphs of the war but Napoleon had begun to withdraw large numbers of French troops from the Peninsula in preparation for his ill-fated attack on Russia. Unfortunately, the optimism was to be sadly misplaced. In September Wellington made his way north-east to undertake the siege of the castle of Burgos perched high on a hill overlooking the town. Burgos was not the sort of fortified town found at Ciudad Rodrigo or Badajoz and, indeed, the castle was relatively small and apparently easy game for the Allies

The Fonseca Colegio at Salamanca. It was from here that Dr Patrick Curtis ran his network of spies during the Peninsular War.

However, Wellington left behind him the 3rd, 4th, 5th and Light Divisions, his veteran storming divisions, and chose to attack the castle with troops from the 1st Division who had pleaded with him to be allowed to show what they could do. Sadly, his decision went against him and the combination of inexperienced troops, the usual lack of siege tools and, more significantly a woeful lack of heavy guns – he undertook the siege with just three heavy guns – resulted in his only major failure of the war.

From start to finish the siege was little short of a fiasco and, apart from the successful storming of the hornwork of San Miguel, prior to the siege proper beginning, there was little to cheer during the month-long episode. The various assaults went in piecemeal and were all thrust back by the French defenders – during an assault on 4 October, the French even obtained a copy of Wellington's plans for the assault from a dead British officer – and, on 8 October, Edward Cocks, a great favourite of Wellington's and an officer of great promise, was killed whilst helping to repulse a French sortie. Wellington wept at Cocks' funeral and with his death it is said that Wellington's heart went out of the siege. Finally, on 21 October, the Allied army packed up and departed for Madrid, ironically, three days after Napoleon began his own retreat at Moscow. The ensuing terrible retreat by Wellington and his army did not end until they had reached Ciudad Rodrigo and the Portuguese border after what Wellington himself called, 'the worst scrape I ever was in.' Indeed, many of those who had experienced both the retreats to Corunna and Burgos said afterwards that the latter was by far the worse. 1812, therefore, a year begun with such a burst of energy, ended as a damp squib.

It should be remembered, however, that the two key fortresses of Ciudad Rodrigo and Badajoz were still in Allied hands and throughout the winter of 1812-13 and the following spring, Wellington's men recovered, reinforcements arrived from England and by May the army was ready to begin its great advance from Portugal into Spain, and the campaign which would see the

The great cathedral at Burgos.

decisive battle of the Peninsular War – Vitoria – and end with Wellington and the Allies poised for the invasion of France.

Throughout the six years of Britain's involvement in the Iberian Peninsula they had received vital support from the Spanish guerrillas whose part in the war Wellington later freely acknowledged. They were a real thorn in the flesh for successive French commanders-in-chief whose resources were drained by having to keep a continual watch over their shoulders for guerrilla activity. By the time of the Vitoria campaign, King Joseph was forced to send escorts of up to 1,500 men in order to ensure that his despatches reached Paris, manpower that he could ill-afford. Indeed, such was the omnipresent threat from these covert killers that the various French armies could never concentrate against Wellington, for had they been able to do so his position in the Peninsula would have become untenable. Instead, he was able to deal with the French armies separately and by the time they did manage to concentrate, as at Vitoria – where the Armies of the South, the Army of Portugal and the Army of the North combined – his own army had grown both in numbers and in stature to deal with them. One must also remember that the French armies in Spain were armies of occupation and as such had a duty to go hunting these guerrillas, and not just sit back and become penned in like sheep in their respective headquarters. As a result, their resources were stretched to the limit by having to leave occupying forces in major towns and cities, otherwise as soon as they moved on they would find a guerrilla force in their rear. It was a most difficult situation for them. The reputation of these unlikely but most valuable allies has for years been as patriotic heroes, but recent research has shown that this is partly myth, and that although some guerrilla units and their leaders were indeed invaluable to Wellington's war effort – Julian Sanchez's cavalry were converted to regular cavalry at the end of the war, for example – many guerrillas used the war as an excuse simply to rob and take whatever they pleased under the false guise of

The River Zadorra at Vitoria.

patriotism. The real losers at the end of the day were the Iberian people who had to endure both the Allied and French armies, as well as the guerrillas. All parties took what the villagers had to offer, the only difference being that Wellington's men paid for their supplies (usually) whereas both the French and the guerrillas took theirs by force. The end result for the villages was the same; they were left with very little. The Vitoria campaign of 1813 began with General Foy's troops, away in the north of Spain, engaged in such a hunt for guerrillas, something which was to prevent him from joining Joseph at Vitoria, and as the war entered the Pyrenees and Navarre, Spanish guerrillas who had been quite active there throughout the war stepped up their operations. Their efforts were, as Wellington later said, an important factor in his eventual triumph.

The Vitoria campaign began with a touch of real theatre from Wellington who, on crossing the Portuguese border, turned in his saddle and said, 'Farewell Portugal, I shall never see you again.' He never

did. The campaign involved an Allied advance in four columns, not along the great high road to France, but north of it, outflanking each successive French position as they went. In this way, strong French positions on the Douro and Esla rivers were turned without having to fight at all. It was a tremendous achievement, and was one conducted in great secrecy for the French never really knew where the main Allied army was until it had passed them. Even Burgos, the great stumbling block in 1812, was avoided, the French abandoning the castle after blowing it up on 14 June. Eventually, the Allied columns converged to the west and north-west of Vitoria on 19 June, ready to do battle. King Joseph's armies had converged on Vitoria some days before, with a huge convoy of accumulated treasure, paintings, gold and silver, accompanying them, as did an astonishing array of non-fighting personnel, of camp followers, French civilian and ministerial staff, wives and *afrancesados*, the pro-French Spaniards who had thrown in their lot with the enemy.

Top, A view looking south towards the heights of Puebla at Vitoria, as seen from the third French position between Zuazo and Crispiana. *Above,* the bridge over the Zadorra at Villodas.

Top, a view of the heights of Puebla from the knoll of Arinez, looking south-west.
Above, the bridge over the Zadorra at Tres Puentes, crossed by Kempt's brigade during the battle.

The bridge over the Zadorra at Tres Puentes. Kempt's brigade crossed this bridge from left to right during the Battle of Vitoria.

On the morning of 21 June Wellington's troops burst from the hills surrounding the valley of the Zadorra, the river which winds its way along the horseshoe valley floor, over which the deciding battle of the war was to be fought. Wellington was trusting much to his subordinates, Hill, Graham, Picton and Dalhousie, particularly the latter two whose instructions were to feel their way into the action depending on events unfolding on their respective right flanks. For a commander rarely used to delegating, Wellington was placing a huge responsibility on their shoulders and, indeed, things did not quite come off as planned. They did work well enough, however, for

Wellington to achieve one of his greatest victories, a victory which looked likely from the moment Hill's 2nd Division began driving the French along the summit of the heights of Puebla on the French left, to open the battle. By 10am Graham's column had cut the main road to Bayonne, thus preventing the possibility of any direct escape to France and when Picton's 3rd Division stormed the bridge of Mendoza in the early afternoon, Joseph's prospects became decidedly bleak. The French were driven from successive positions after severe fighting but when Gazan abandoned his position on the French left Joseph's army gave way and there followed unprecedented

sent by Wellington to the Prince Regent who in turn made him Britain's first Field Marshal.

Wellington, however, was in no mood for such niceties on the evening of 21 June and morning of 22 June for, as at Salamanca, he had seen the French army escape his clutches once again, this time due to the plundering of the French baggage train. It was this episode which moved him to refer to his men as 'the scum of the earth' in a despatch to Lord Bathurst. This was slightly unfair to a large part of the army, however, for whole regiments of infantry and cavalry saw none of the treasure, forming up and pitching camp to the north of the town following the battle itself and as such taking no part in the disgraceful aftermath. But few could blame the men. Arrears of pay were commonplace in

launch a fine counter-attack in the Pyrenees the following month, as well as ensuring that Wellington would have a fight on his hands when he invaded France towards the end of the year.

The great victory on 21 June had far reaching consequences for, even as the battle was being fought, Napoleon had negotiated a treaty with the Austrians, Russians and Prussians. The consequences of the outcome of the battle of Vitoria were not lost on Napoleon who tried his best to suppress the news from both the Austrians and Prussians. He was unsuccessful, however, and on 21 August the treaty was repudiated and hostilities broke out once again. Vitoria, therefore, can be said to be one of the most decisive and important battles of the Napoleonic period.

King Joseph, and Marshals Junot, Victor, Massena

was not helped by the ineptitude of Gazan. This, coupled with the fact that the French army was now fighting not as an army of occupation but as an army about to defend its homeland, made Soult's job far easier than it might otherwise have been and as he fell back, his position, ironically, became stronger as he was retreating upon his base, namely Bayonne.

Soult's first counter-attack came on 25 July, the first day of what was known as the battle of the Pyrenees, a series of actions which lasted until 2 August. Why Soult gave up the passes at Maya and Roncesvalles, and then attacked them is slightly puzzling but that was his course of action, and when he attacked these two passes on Sunday, 25 July, ostensibly an attempt to relieve the garrison of Pamplona, he was partially successful, particularly at Maya where troops from Hill's 2nd Division were driven along the ridge which runs east of the pass and down into the valley of the Baztan. D'Erlon, commanding the French, chose not to press down in pursuit, however, and save for the capture of the pass itself, little was gained strategically by the French. A different and far more serious situation occurred at Roncesvalles, however, where Cole was attacked on the same day by Clausel and Reille. His men held the French in check for most of the day until dense fog brought the curtain down on the day's fighting. Unnerved by this, and fearing the French might get around his flank, he pulled back and withdrew his men south. When Wellington, who was away to the west at Lesaca during the day, heard about this he was not too perturbed as there was a good defensive position at Zubiri, a few miles to the south. Unfortunately, Cole, who

had been joined by Picton, had completely lost his nerve and fell back far beyond there, to the village of Sorauren, almost at the gates of Pamplona, much to Wellington's great dismay and in direct disobedience to his orders. Cole and Picton may have been great fighters and the latter, in particular, one of the army's real firebrands, but, as Wellington said, 'when I am obliged to quit them they are children.'

Wellington finally joined Cole at Sorauren on 27 July and, after narrowly avoiding capture by French cavalry as he coolly dictated an order to Fitzroy Somerset, he rode up alone in front of his men to assume command. The first troops he came upon were Portuguese who, since May 1809, had called him 'Douro' and it was this shout that now went up. It must have been one of the memorable moments of the war as the chant, 'Douro! Douro!' rang out, a cry taken up in turn by each British regiment as it rolled along the mountainside from left to right. The effect of this chanting must have been as inspiring to the Allies as it was disheartening to the French. Indeed, observing the effect it had upon his men, Wellington, who usually disliked such worshipping – 'if they cheer you one day, they may turn against you the next', he claimed – indulged it, and when he peered through his telescope across the valley at Soult he saw a man who knew his chance had gone. Wellington spent the wet and stormy night of 27 July wrapped in his cloak upon the hillside along with his men. By the end of the Napoleonic Wars such a storm would become the omen of victory for Wellington's men, preceding as they did the great victories at Vitoria, Salamanca and Waterloo.

San Sebastian has changed enormously since 1813. The River Urumea has been canalised and the old walls removed. The British and Portuguese stormers would have attacked across the estuary and river, which is now difficult to imagine. The tree-covered Monte Urgullo, to where Rey's garrison retreated after the storming on 31 August, can be seen in the background.

The Crossing of the Bidassoa took place here on 7 October 1813, with the Foot Guards and King's German Legion crossing the river here from left to right. Foy burned the old bridge that once stood here after his retreat following the Battle of Vitoria. In the background can be seen the San Marcial heights, scene of the Spanish victory of 31 August 1813.

Wellington's headquarters throughout the winter of 1813-14 were here in the Rue Mazarin, in St Jean de Luz.

Soult's main attack was duly delivered on 28 July in the usual style, dense blue columns ascending the steep hills on which the Allies were positioned. All credit must be given to the French throughout the Pyrenees campaign for the stamina they showed in even attempting to force the Allied line, for as at Roncesvalles and, to a lesser extent, Maya, they had to negotiate long and difficult marches before they could finally engage Wellington's men. At Sorauren the fighting was hard and on the Allied left inroads were made in their line. But French successes were short-lived and they were thrown back at bayonet point by determined Allied counter-attacks. The battle subsided into stalemate and both armies remained where they were throughout 29 July, during which further British reinforcements arrived, and when Soult moved on the 30th he was attacked with great vigour by Wellington and driven back over the mountains into France. His attempt to relieve Pamplona had ended in failure.

Whilst the hard fighting in the Pyrenees had been going on, Sir Thomas Graham had been busy supervising at the siege of San Sebastian, the third of Wellington's great bloody sieges in the Peninsula. Once again, the operation was unsatisfactory and the first assault on the place, on 25 July, failed. On 31 August another assault was made, in broad daylight, and in full view of hundreds of spectators who came from the surrounding towns and villages to watch. The Allied troops ran the gauntlet of fire across the shallow waters of the Urumea river to attack the breaches made in the sea wall but the attack stalled, held up by determined French resistance, until Graham gave orders for his guns to open fire over the heads of the attacking troops and on to the French defenders. This innovation worked to perfection, to which the line of headless French bodies testified. British and Portuguese troops pressed their faces into the rocks whilst a stream of shells smashed into the defenders, driving them back and allowing the Allies to finally enter the town. General Rey, commanding the garrison, pulled his

Previous pages. It is easy to see why the battlefields of the Pyrenees and the Nivelle are the most spectacular in the Peninsula. *Page 78*, a view looking south-west from the Rhune, towards the Bayonet Ridge, the eastern side of which is marked by the line of duty-free shops. *Page 79*, the spur running off the main ridge at Maya. It was here that Pringle's brigade and, in particular, the 28th, had such a desperate time on 25 July 1813.

The Napoleonic fort atop the Linduz Plateau, Roncesvalles. In the far distance can be seen the Leizar Atheca, the scene of fierce fighting on 25 July 1813.

men back to the safety of the castle at the top of Monte Urgull, where they surrendered on 7 September. Once again, sadly, there followed the usual scenes of disorder as the town was sacked, the rioting made all the worse by a fire which all but destroyed the old town. Many considered the aftermath at San Sebastian to have been worse than Badajoz, which may be true. Perhaps the many diarists of the day had exhausted themselves during that particular episode and, to prevent repetition, said merely that San Sebastian was as bad, and made worse than Badajoz by the fire. The Spaniards themselves added to the controversy by claiming that Wellington himself had ordered the town to be put to the torch as a penalty for the town's continued trading with nearby France, a notion scoffed at with indignity by him. Indeed, Wellington held an internal enquiry into the cause of the fire, after which he was perfectly satisfied that his men had done no wrong.

With San Sebastian taken, only Pamplona remained in French hands. There was, of course, a French army under the redoubtable Marshal Suchet still operating on the east coast of Spain, and for a while Wellington considered moving east against them. However, he chose to push on to the French border, leaving Pamplona to be blockaded rather than besieged in the regular manner. Pamplona eventually fell to the jubilant Spaniards on 25 October 1813. As a result, Suchet was forced to relinquish his tenuous hold in Catalonia and withdraw towards the Pyrenees, crossing back over the French border in late 1813 with just 15,000 men.

On the very day that San Sebastian fell to the Allies, Soult launched what was to be the last battle fought by the French army in Spain, the ill-fated San Marcial offensive of 31 August. This was Soult's last-ditched attempt to relieve San Sebastian but, like the battle of the Pyrenees which was intended to relieve Pamplona, it failed. Soult's men crossed the Bidassoa river to attack the Spanish troops at the top of the steep heights opposite. The battle saw one of the few occasions where, having learned from their British comrades, the Spanish troops waited patiently at the top instead of

Part of the French defences that still remain on the Lesser Rhune.

back in the summer of 1808.

By the first week of October Wellington was poised to begin his long-awaited invasion of France. Facing him along a sixteen-mile front were just 47,000 French troops, thinly spread and concentrated around the lofty mountain, La Rhune, which dominates the whole area. There were close to 15,000 French troops in this sector with a further 14,000 troops away to the east. Just 10,000 troops defended the sector between the Rhune and the Atlantic as this area was considered to be impassable and the least likely target of Wellington's main thrust. Unfortunately for Soult, Wellington planned to attack this very same front. He gave orders for diversionary movements to be made away to the east while several smaller ruses were staged with the intention of deceiving the French. Indeed, he himself rode to Roncesvalles to visit the 6th Division and made sure that the French knew he was there. It was all intended to tease, torment and badger the French into believing that the invasion would be made over the hills and tracks around La Rhune.

charging down at the enemy. The result was that, as the French neared the top of the heights the Spaniards opened fire before rushing at the French and driving them back at bayonet point. That the French troops noticed large red columns waiting silently behind the Spaniards perhaps had something to do with their less than vigorous attack but little should be taken away from the Spaniards and their commanding officer, Bernadin Freire, who at one stage of the battle appealed to Wellington for British help. But Wellington, now observing that the French were as good as beaten, refused, saying, 'if I send you the English troops you ask for, they will win the battle; but as the French are already in retreat you may as well win it for yourselves.' The result was a belated win for the Spanish army, which had enjoyed few successes since their victory over the French at Baylen

Previous pages; the two redoubts covering the southern approaches to Sare, during the Battle of the Nivelle. *Page 82*, the Grenade Redoubt, and, *Page 83*, the Sainte Barbe Redoubt.

At about 7.30 on the morning of 7 October the red trail of a rocket sent spiralling into the grey morning sky signalled the beginning of the Allied invasion of France. The 1st and 5th Divisions stepped off from their positions on the southern bank and began crossing the Bidassoa, local shrimpers leading the way to guide the Allied troops across the shallow estuary. By 11.30 Wellington's men were firmly in possession of the northern bank having driven back the French defenders who retired to another position further north. The fighting was fiercer above Vera, where the Light Division attacked French positions on the Bayonet Ridge, but by the early afternoon they were in possession of all their objectives. More important, the French defenders on the Rhune, faced with being cut off from the main French positions, withdrew across the ravine which divides the Rhune from the Lesser Rhune and took up positions behind walls and amidst the rocky crags of the latter's razor-backed crest.

Later that same afternoon, Wellington perhaps contemplated

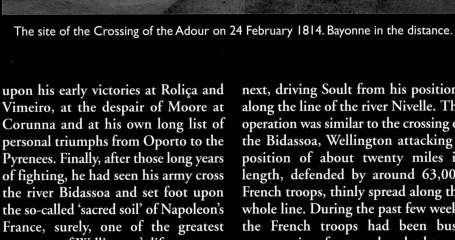

The site of the Crossing of the Adour on 24 February 1814. Bayonne in the distance.

upon his early victories at Roliça and Vimeiro, at the despair of Moore at Corunna and at his own long list of personal triumphs from Oporto to the Pyrenees. Finally, after those long years of fighting, he had seen his army cross the river Bidassoa and set foot upon the so-called 'sacred soil' of Napoleon's France, surely, one of the greatest moments of Wellington's life.

There was a lull of just under a month before Wellington struck

next, driving Soult from his positions along the line of the river Nivelle. The operation was similar to the crossing o the Bidassoa, Wellington attacking a position of about twenty miles in length, defended by around 63,000 French troops, thinly spread along the whole line. During the past few weeks the French troops had been busy constructing forts and redoubts or most of the more prominent hilltops to create a strong position which

Some relics of the Peninsular War have, sadly, succumbed to the elements during the passing of the years. Take the bridge of Amotz, for example, the only lateral communication between the French left and centre during the Battle of the Nivelle, seen above a few years ago and, *right*, after the flash flood of March 2007.

ICI REPOSA PENDANT 46 ANS
LE CORPS DU GÉNÉRAL DE DIVISION
LUBIN MARTIN VAN DER MAËSEN
MORT AU CHAMP D'HONNEUR
LE 1 SEPTEMBRE 1813
AU PASSAGE DE LA BIDASSOA
SUR LE PONT DE BÉRA

SOUVENIR ET HOMMAGE DE RECONNAISSANCE
DE LA FAMILLE DU GÉNÉRAL
A LA COMMUNE D'ASCAIN

Left to right, the church at Arcangues, the scene of the 43rd's fight during the Battle of the Nive. The inside of the church at Arcangues. The bridge at Vera, defended by Daniel Cadoux and his company of the 95th Rifles on 31 August 1813.

would have to be attacked frontally by Wellington. His plan was a reverse of that employed during the Bidassoa operation. On this occasion, Hope's 1st and 5th Divisions, along with two Spanish divisions, were to tease the enemy on its right, close to the Atlantic. The main Allied attacks, however, were to be launched in the centre against the Rhune and between Sare and the bridge over the Nivelle at Amotz. Hill was to attack the French left at the same time.

The Battle of the Nivelle was fought on 10 November 1813, and proved yet another great success for Wellington and his army who swept all before them, driving the French from their forts after some stiff fighting in many places. The great chronicler of the Peninsular War, William Napier, present during the attack on the Lesser Rhune, wrote, 'The plains of France so long overlooked from the towering crags of the Pyrenees were to be the prize of the battle, and the half-famished soldiers in their fury, broke through the iron barrier erected by Soult as if it were but a screen of reeds.' Indeed,

The church at Guethary, a British telegraph station throughout the winter of 1813-14.

by the end of the day Soult had been driven back upon Bayonne, his main base. For Soult, the battle had been another disaster, although ironically his position still grew stronger as he fell back upon Bayonne, with the river Nive on his left flank and the Atlantic on his right, a narrow front defended in depth by his men. For Wellington it was a different story. He had seen his army achieve yet another great victory and even though he was never one to lavish praise upon his men he was moved to call his army, 'probably the most complete machine for its numbers now existing in Europe.' High praise indeed, but justified.

A further four weeks passed before the two armies next clashed, on 9 December, the first day of the four-day battle of the Nive. Soult was firmly pinned against Bayonne and the river Ardour, but he had the great advantage of being able to operate either to the left or right of the river Nive, which ran due south from Bayonne, by virtue of the bridges in the city. Wellington, on the other hand, had divided his force, Hill taking the eastern or right bank of the

A view looking east at Orthes, with the main French position lying just beyond the trees. The 3rd Division, supported by the 6th Division, attacked up the slopes from right to left.

The beautiful medieval bridge over the Gave de Pau at Orthes. Despite its relative lack of coverage in histories of the war, Orthes remains the only battle in which Wellington was wounded.

Nive whilst Wellington occupied the west or left bank of the river with his left flank resting upon the Atlantic. Hill crossed the Nive on 9 December, his intention being to threaten Soult's retreat to the east and the interior of France. However, on 10 December Soult counter-attacked and drove back Wellington's left flank for almost three miles, the centre of the latter's army – the Light Division – being driven back to Arcangues, where it halted the retirement. The main French attacks were thwarted, but this did not deter them for Soult persisted in his pushes on 11 and 12 December but to little avail.

The main action came on 13 December, a battle since known as the Battle of St Pierre. The pontoon bridge linking Wellington and Hill was washed away by heavy rains, thereby isolating Hill on the right bank of the Nive. Soult was able, therefore, to transfer his men to that side and attack, knowing that he had about four hours to defeat Hill before the pontoon was restored and before reinforcements arrived from Ustaritz, the next crossing point south on the Nive. The action began at 8am, when Soult's columns loomed out of the morning gloom to begin their attack. The next four hours saw some extremely hard fighting as Hill strove to maintain his position, throwing in most of his reserves in the face of determined French attacks. Fortunately, Wellington's most trusted subordinate proved more than capable of winning the battle before Wellington arrived with reinforcements. Hill, in fact, chose to close the battle with the men under his command and as the commander-in-chief rode up he declared Hill the victor, declining to take command and adding, 'My dear Hill, the day's your own.'

The year of 1813 ended with Wellington firmly established in southern France and with the great French military base of Bayonne in his grip. Indeed, on 23 February 1814 the vice was further tightened when his men crossed the river Adour and began blockading the town from the north, by which time Soult had retreated east, leaving around 14,000 French troops to garrison the town. On 27 February Wellington's army fought its last major battle in open ground amidst the green, lush slopes of the main Dax-Orthes road. There was little stopping the Allied army at this stage of the war and when its columns ascended the long, gradual slopes to attack the enemy they were triumphant once again, the French putting up a stiff fight at the village of St Boes but not stiff enough to stop the Allied juggernaut.

The pursuit of Soult's army took Wellington to Toulouse, where he arrived during the closing week of March, his men fighting a couple of sharp actions along the way at Aire and Tarbes. It is quite ironic that such a satisfactory war – from Wellington's point of view – should come to such an unsatisfactory finale with the messy and bloody assault on Toulouse on 10 April 1814. Over 4,500 Allied troops became casualties by the end of a day which saw them clear the French from their positions along the Calvinet Ridge, against 3,200 French casualties. The result of the battle gave Wellington his final triumph – albeit a kind of pyrrhic one – in the Peninsula. Six long, hard years of fighting were finally over, although the battle need never have been fought at all. Indeed, Napoleon had already abdicated on 6 April, although Wellington was not to receive news of the event until 12 April, two days after the Battle

Opposite, the memorial to the French army on the Dax-Orthes road at Orthes.

ICI REPOSENT DES SOLDATS
FRANCAIS ANGLAIS
PORTUGAIS ESPAGNOLS
BATAILLE D'ORTHEZ
27 FEVRIER 1814

SOUVENIR FRANCAIS
DELEGATION
DES PYRENEES ATLANTIQUES
COMITES
D'ORTHEZ PAU ANGLET
16 MAI 1998

The monument to General Maxmillien Foy, who received the fourteenth wound of his distinguished career at Orthes.

of Toulouse. Soult, in fact, did no accept defeat until 17 April. And ye even though Napoleon had already abdicated and the war, in theory, wa at an end, there was still time for more blood to be shed, the blood of 1,73 Allied and French casualties to be precise during the sortie from Bayonne on the night of 14 Apri when French troops issued from the gates of the citadel on the north bank of the Adour to drive back the British and German troops blockading the town from the north. The French were eventually driven back after a night of fierce, confused fighting leaving Major General Hay dead and Sir John Hope wounded and then captured. For what? The French governor, Thouvenot, claims not to have known about events elsewhere in France but one cannot believe but that the sortie was launched purely out of malice, and as a final, desperate act of a mischievous French soldier.

Not counting the first even which sparked off the Peninsular War – Junot's invasion of Portugal in November 1807 – the war lasted from 1808 until 1814. These six long years

Previous pages, Page 96, the battlefield cemetery at Orthes and *Page 97*, the ford over the Gave de Oloron at Monein, where Picton controversially came to grief on 24 February 1814.

The battlefield of Garris, 15 February 1814, as seen from the French position at the top of the steep slope. Just when his army was preparing to bivouac for the night, Wellington arrived and ordered the hill to be stormed 'before dark.'

The battlefield of Aire, one of Hill's actions fought on 2 March 1814. Hill's infantry attacked up the slopes towards the camera.

The memorial obelisk on the Calvinet Ridge Toulouse, close to the original site of the great redoubt.

of warfare were Britain's greatest contribution to the first downfall of Napoleon and were a constant drain on French manpower and resources. It was no coincidence, in fact, that Napoleon called the war 'the Spanish ulcer', for that is what it was, a 'running sore'. Many consider the war in the Peninsula to have been a mere sideshow when compared to the great campaigns in Russia, Austria and Germany, and perhaps they are right. Wellington was never in a position to threaten Paris strategically, but the Anglo-Portuguese army got a grip of affairs in Spain and Portugal and, along with the Spanish armies and the guerrillas, never really let go. They hung on at times but by the end of 1813 they were across the French border. Similarly, the great battles at Salamanca and Vitoria were never on the scale of Borodino, Austerlitz or Leipzig, but the Austrians, Prussians or

Russians could never claim such a record in the field as Wellington's, in spite of Napoleon sending a succession of tried and tested marshals against him. Wellington defeated them all. And, of course, he defeated Napoleon himself when he finally came face to face with him at Waterloo. Unfortunately, Waterloo has tended to overshadow the achievements of Wellington's Anglo-Portuguese army in the Peninsula, an army which barely lost a gun, let alone a battle, and there are few armies which can boast a similar record. The Peninsular War should, therefore, be considered to be much more than a sideshow, for it was an integral part of the final downfall of the Emperor Napoleon, and if the Battle of Waterloo was won on the playing fields of Eton, then it was on the dusty battlefields of the Peninsula that the seeds of that final victory were sown.

Left, the Canal du Midi, Toulouse, at the Ponts de Jumeux, where Picton's attack failed on 10 April 1814. *Below*, the gravestone of Colonel Forbes, commanding officer of the 45th Foot, killed during the failed attack.

The Coldstream Guards cemetery in Bayonne. Despite its name, officers from other regiments are buried here. All died as a result of the sortie from Bayonne on the night of 14 April 1814.

The 3rd Foot Guards cemetery, Bayonne. This tiny but very poignant cemetery contains the graves of four officers from the 3rd Foot Guards who were killed during the sortie from Bayonne.

To the Glory of God ... To the Glory ... and to the memory of / à la mémoire de

CAPTAIN DANIEL CADOUX ... CAPITAN DANIEL CADOUX
AND HIS GALLANT RIFLEMEN ... DE SES VALEROSOS CAZADORES
OF THE 95TH RIFLE BRIGADE ... DEL REGIMIENTO INGLES
WHO ON 1 SEPTEMBER 1813 ... RIFLE BRIGADE
FELL GLORIOUSLY ... QUE MURIERON DEFENDIENDO
DEFENDING THIS BRIDGE ... ESTE PUENTE EL 1º DE SEPTIEMBRE
AGAINST THE FURIOUS ATTACK ... HEROICAMENTE CONTRA
OF A FRENCH DIVISION ... UNA DIVISION FRANCESA

A
GUILLAUME-JEAN-LYON
LIEUT: AU 14.ME REC: DES DRACONS
BRITANNIQUES QUI FUT TUE
LE 18 MARS 1814. PRÈS
CADILLON À LA RETRAITE
DE L'ARMÉE FRANÇAISE
VERS TOULOUSE.

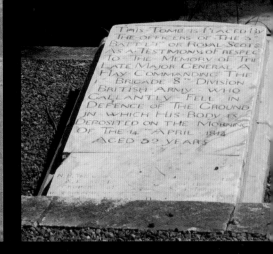

THIS TOMB IS PLACED BY
THE OFFICERS OF THE 3
BATT: 1ST OR ROYAL SCOTS
AS A TESTIMONY OF RESPECT
TO THE MEMORY OF THE
LATE MAJOR GENERAL A
HAY COMMANDING THE
BRIGADE 5TH DIVISION
BRITISH ARMY WHO
GALLANTLY FELL IN
DEFENCE OF THE GROUND
IN WHICH HIS BODY IS
DEPOSITED ON THE MORNING
OF THE 14TH APRIL 1814
AGED 59 YEARS

MAJOR GENERAL ROBERT CRAUFURD

HONNEUR — PATRIE

A LA MÉMOIRE DU
Général de Brigade BÉCHAUD
DES OFFICIERS, SOUS OFFICIERS ET SOLDATS
DE L'ARMÉE DU MARÉCHAL SOULT
tués à la Défense de Saint-Boès
bataille d'Orthez 27 Février 1814

A NOUS LE SOUVENIR À EUX L'IMMORTALITÉ !

SOCIÉTÉ NATIONALE
DU
SOUVENIR FRANÇAIS

TROUPES DE LA DEFENSE

GENERAL DE DIVISION baron THOUVENOT Commandant en chef
GENERAL DE DIVISION baron ABBE
GENERAUX DE BRIGADE SOL-BEAUCLAIR baron BERGE baron GARBE
MAUCOMBLE, BEURET DELORME

1ER BATAILLON DES 1E 63E 66E 70E 82E — 1ER ET 2E BATAILLONS DES 26E 64E 94E
1ER ET 3E BATAILLONS DU 95E — 2E ET 3E BATAILLONS DU 119E
3E BATAILLON DU 120E — 4E BATAILLON DU 118E
REGIMENTS D'INFANTERIE DE LIGNE

1ER BATAILLON DES 5E 27E — 4E BATAILLON DES 31E 34E
REGIMENTS D'INFANTERIE LEGERE

SEPT C.IES DES 3E 5E 6E 8E REGIMENTS D'ARTILLERIE A PIED
2E BATAILLON DE SAPEURS (3E ET 9E C.IES)
COMPAGNIE DES PIONNIERS DE BAYONNE (4E C.IE)
1ER BATAILLON DE PONTONNIERS (4E C.IE)
DETACHEMENT DU 15E REGIMENT DE CHASSEURS A CHEVAL
GARDE NATIONALE — GENDARMERIE

12E EQUIPAGE DE FLOTTILLE

... ENTO MIDDLESEX ... HERE LIE THE COLOURS
... JE DE CAMBRIDGE) ... OF THE 57TH AND 77TH
... REGIMENTS OF FOOT
SE ENCUENTRAN ... LATER THE MIDDLESEX REGIMENT
... ADAS LAS BANDERAS ... (DUKE OF CAMBRIDGE'S OWN)
... S REGIMIENTOS 57 Y 77 ... WHICH WERE CARRIED IN BATTLE
... INFANTERIA BRITANICA ... BETWEEN
... PORTARON EN BATALLA ... 1853 - 1876
ENTRE
1853 Y 1876

JOHN BERESFORD ...
... Reg ...
by the explosion of a Mine ...
breach at Ciudad Rodrigo ...
19th January 1812

O T.te JOÃO BERESFORD do
Reg.to N.o 88 p.lo effeito d'huma
Mina que voou na brecha de
Ciudad Rodrigo, e que elle entre
os premeiros montou ena noite
de 19 d Janeiro 1812
morreo na edade de 21 annos

S.BOS Marquez de campo Maior
de este modo mandou commemorar
a morte d'hum parente estimado

SACRED TO THE MEMORY
OF THE UNDER NAMED OFFICERS
WHO GALLANTLY FELL ...
... GARRISON
... BAYONNE
ON THE ...

COLDSTREAM GUARDS
LIEUT ...
... MAJOR ...

... W. G. CROFTON
BURROUGHS ADJ.T
ENSIGNS

1ST REGT OF GUARDS
ENSIGN
... LANE
... OF CHARLES
... PATES
... LIEUT J. B. SKIFFNER
LIEUT
... OURNE ADJ.T

60TH REG.T
LIEUT
J. BARLTON

THIS TABLET
WAS PLACED TO THE MEMORY OF THE
ABOVE NAMED OFFICERS BY THEIR
FRIEND AND COMPANION AT THE SORTIE

DE CETTE HAUTEUR
... ET REPRISE A LA BATAILLE DE SAINT PIERRE D'IRUBE
... DEFENSE SUR LES MONTAGNES ET LES VALLÉES DU PAYS BASQUE
AVEC DES FORCES INFERIEURES PIED A PIED
LE MARÉCHAL SOULT
DUC DE DALMATIE, LIEUTENANT DE L'EMPEREUR
... DEFENDIT CE PAYS PENDANT SEPT MOIS
CONTRE L'ARMÉE DE WELLINGTON

1813 - 1814

BURIAL PLACE OF THE BRITISH OFFICERS
ESPECIALLY OF THE COLDSTREAM GUARDS
WHO FELL IN ACTION NEAR TO THIS SPOT
... 14th OF APRIL ... THE NIGHT OF THE
SORTIE FROM THE CITADEL OF BAYONNE
...
...

THIS GROUND WAS PURCHASED BY THE
GUARDS IN 1814. RESTORED BY THEM IN
1830 AND 1858. IT WAS PUT INTO ITS
PRESENT SHAPE BY MISS HOLBURNE OF
BATH A.D. 1875

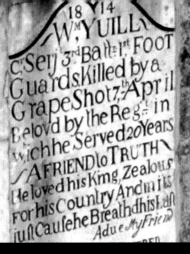

18 14
Wm YUILL
... SERJt 3rd Battn 1st FOOT
Guards Killed by a
Grape Shot 7 April
Belovd by the Regt in
wich he Served 20 Years
A FRIEND to TRUTH
He loved his King, Zealous
For his Country And its
just Cause he Breath'd his last
Adue My Friend

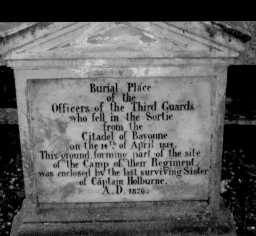

Burial Place
of the
Officers of the Third Guards
who fell in the Sortie
from the
Citadel of Bayonne
on the 14th of April 1814.
This ground, forming part of the site
of the Camp of their Regiment,
was enclosed by the last surviving Sister
of Captain Holburne.
A.D. 1876.

POSTO DE COMANDO DO MARECHAL GENERAL
ARTHUR WELLESLEY, DUQUE DE WELLINGTON
COMANDANTE EM CHEFE DAS FORÇAS
ANGLO-LUSAS NA BATALHA DO BUÇACO

TRAVADA EM 27 DE SETEMBRO DE 1810
COLOCADA EM 27-X-1947

KINGS GERMAN LEGION

LT KLANCK,	BIDASSOA OCT.7.
LT GEO. SCHARTORIUS, BCK.. LT INFY	NIVELLE NOV.10.
LT GEO. BOYD,	NIVELLE NOV.10.
CAPT E. DE. BRAXION, BCK..O.E.L.S.	ORTHEZ FEB. 27.
LT E. KOSCHENAHR, BCK..O.E.L.S.	ORTHEZ FEB. 27.
LT C. MILLINS, CHASSEURS BRITTANIQUES,	ORTHEZ FEB. 27.
MAJ. LYMPHER, R.H. ARTILLERY.	ORTHEZ FEB. 27.
LT ED BLUMENBACH, R.H. ARTILLERY.	TOULOUSE APL.10.
MAJ. PAUL CLUDEN,	BAYONNE APL.14.
CAPT H. MÜLLER,	BAYONNE APL.14.
LT J. MEYLER,	BAYONNE APL.14.
LT C. KOHLER,	BAYONNE APL.14.

N.C.O. .. I OCT.7. .. I FEB.27..11 APL.14.
DRS.. 11 NOV.10.
R.F. XVII OCT.7. .. XX NOV.10. .. V DEC.9.

... HERE REPOSE THE ...
... MORTAL REMAINS OF ...
... JOHN HILL 2d Lieut Co...
... WHO FELL ... ENGL...
... AGED 24 YEARS ...

... CHAMP D'HONNEUR DANS LES
... BATAILLES DE LA NIVE LES 10 11 ET 12 DÉCRE 18..
... ENSEVELIS DANS CET ...
... mark the resting place of brave m...
This ... was placed here by
Lt Colonel W. Hill JAMES
(Late 31st Regiment)
April 1897
... the 60th year of
the reign of ...

A LA MÉMOIRE
... COLONEL RICKARD LLOY...
... COMBAT DE LA NIVE, LE 10E DÉCEMBRE 1...
... TÊTE DU 84E RÉGIMENT D'INFANTERIE ANGLA...
... ÂGÉ DE 37 ANS.
... admiré et respecté par sa Patrie reconnaissan...
... honoré et estimé par ses Officiers, et ses Sold...
... chéri et regretté par ses nombreux Amis

Memorial to the defenders of Bayonne and to the sortie of 14 April 1814.

Bibliography

The early years of the Napoleonic Wars yielded few memoirs or diaries by British soldiers – understandably, given the lack of British military success during this period. In contrast, the Peninsular War was barely a year old when the first accounts began to appear, and by the end of the war in 1814 memoirs of the campaigns were attracting a wide readership. While the war was in progress scores of soldiers unsurprisingly wrote detailed letters to their friends and families in Britain. Most were not made public until long after the war had ended – and, even today, almost every year sees the appearance of previously unpublished material. Such letters – and similar journals – are among the most valuable sources, since they provide a record of events as they unfolded, without the benefit of hindsight or the consciousness of a reading public's expectations. As the great Peninsular historian Sir Charles Oman observed in his *Wellington's Army* (1913), a soldier writing about the retreat to Corunna after the war had ended did so with the knowledge that battles such as Salamanca, Vitoria, and even Waterloo were to follow, whereas the man describing Corunna in the winter of 1808–9 had no such cause for optimism.

The first years after the Napoleonic Wars saw even more memoirs published, including *The Subaltern* by George Gleig (1825), John Green's *Vicissitudes of a Soldier's Life* (1827) and Moyle Sherer's *Recollections of the Peninsula* (1827). But this steady flow of first-hand accounts and reminiscences became a flood in 1828 following the publication of the first volume of Sir William Napier's classic and indispensable *History of the War in the Peninsula and in the South of France, from the Year 1807 to the Year 1814*. Napier, himself a veteran of the Peninsular campaigns with the 43rd Light Infantry, inspired many officers and men to write their own versions of events. Among the finest to appear during the years in which Napier's volumes were being published are John Cooke's *Memoirs of the Late War* (1831), Jonathan Leach's *Rough Sketches of the Life of an Old Soldier* (1831), William Surtees's *Twenty-Five Years in the Rifle Brigade* (1833), Charles Cadell's *Narrative of the Campaigns of the Twenty-Eighth Regiment* (1835), and, perhaps the most famous of all, John Kincaid's *Adventures in the Rifle Brigade* (1831).

Wellington's men were relatively young at the time of the Peninsular and Waterloo campaigns, and by the 1830s and early 1840s could still accurately recall the events of 1808–15. By the 1850s, however, their memories were beginning to fade. Some veterans described events which they could not possibly have witnessed, basing their accounts on the recollections of comrades or, as was increasingly the case, on the pages of Napier's *History*. This does not necessarily devalue them – many contain nuggets of authentic experience – but one should be wary of what might be called the 'Napier factor' when reading memoirs that were written after the mid-1840s. Nevertheless, the post-Napier years did see the publication of such gems as John Spencer Cooper's *Rough Notes of Seven Campaigns, 1809–1815* (1869). While some of the now ageing veterans dictated their memoirs to be published posthumously –

Benjamin Harris's *Recollections* (1829) is perhaps the best known – others left behind papers with family, friends or their old regiments: for example, Augustus Frazer's *Letters* (1859), William Lawrence's *Autobiography* (1886), William Tomkinson's *Diary of a Cavalry Officer* (1894), and William Grattan's *Adventures with the Connaught Rangers* (1902). Although Wellington himself never systematically recorded his experiences in the Peninsula or at Waterloo, we do however have the twelve substantial volumes of his *Despatches*, which also contain many of the orders issued by Wellington to his army, and the fifteen volumes of *Supplementary Despatches*, which collect together much of his incoming correspondence. Beautifully written and models of clarity, the despatches provide a unique insight into Wellington's character, demonstrating the minute detail in which he addressed an astonishing array of matters relating to the war, the army, the Allied governments and regencies, throughout his campaigns. On a typical day he can be found writing to a Major General Peacocke, to the governor of Lisbon, twice to the Earl of Liverpool, the Secretary of State for War, and to General Sir Rowland Hill, one of the most trusted of his subordinates, concerning such topics as the movement of troops, their payment, their diseases, the appointment of officers, and the overall strategic situation in the Peninsula. Even the French generals and marshals who faced him in the field found themselves the recipients of his missives on more than one occasion. These various sources have produced a rich vein of military literature, which all subsequent historians have gratefully mined ever since the Napoleonic wars ended in 1815.

William Napier, of the 43rd Light Infantry. A veteran of the Peninsular War and author of the six-volume *History of the War in the Peninsula and in the South of France* (London, 1828-45)

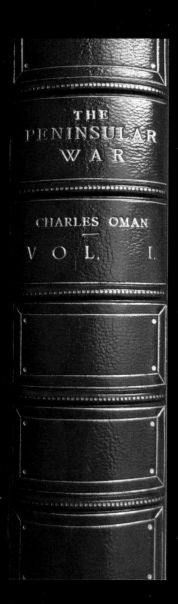

Aitchison, J., *An Ensign in the Peninsular War: the Letters of John Aitchison*, ed. W. F. K. Thompson (London, 1981).

Anderson, J., *Recollections of a Peninsular Veteran* (London, 1913).

Anglesey, Marquess of, *One Leg: the Life and Letters of Henry William Paget, First Marquess of Anglesey* (London, 1961).

Beatson, Major General F. *Wellington: the Bidassoa and the Nivelle* (London, 1935).

———, *Wellington: the Crossing of the Gaves and the Battle of Orthes* (London, 1925).

———, *With Wellington in the Pyrenees* (London, 1914).

Blakiston, J., *Twelve Years' Military Adventure in Three Quarters of the Globe* (London, 1829).

Boutflower, Charles., *The Journal of an Army Surgeon during the Peninsular War* (Manchester, 1912).

Bragge, W., *Peninsular Portrait, 1811–1814: the Letters of Captain William Bragge, Third (King's Own) Dragoons*, ed. S. A. C. Cassells (London, 1963).

Brett-James, A. *Life in Wellington's Army* (London, 1972).

Buckham, E. W., *Personal Narrative of Adventures in the Peninsula during the War in 1812–1813* (London, 1827).

Burgoyne, Sir J., *Life and Correspondence*, ed. C. Wrottesley (2 vols, London, 1873).

Clark-Kennedy, A. E., *Attack the Colour! The Royal Dragoons in the Peninsula and at Waterloo* (London, 1975).

Clerk, Reverend A., *Memoir of Colonel John Cameron, Fassiefern* (Glasgow, 1858).

Cole, M. L. and Gwynn, S., *Memoirs of Sir Lowry Cole*,(London, 1934).

Colville, John., *Portrait of a General: a Chronicle of the Napoleonic Wars* (London, 1980).

Combermere, Viscount, *Memoirs and Correspondence of Field Marshal Viscount Combermere, G.C.B.* (2 vols, London, 1866).

Craufurd, A., *General Craufurd and his Light Division* (London, 1891).

Dallas, A., *Autobiography of the Rev. Alexander Dallas, Including His Service in the Peninsula in the Commissariat Department* (London, 1870).

Daniel, J. E., *Journal of an Officer in the Commissariat Department of the Army* (London, 1820).

Delavoye, A. M., *Life of Thomas Graham, Lord Lynedoch* (London, 1880).

Dickson, A., *The Dickson Manuscripts, 1809–1818*, ed. J. H. Leslie (Woolwich, 1905).

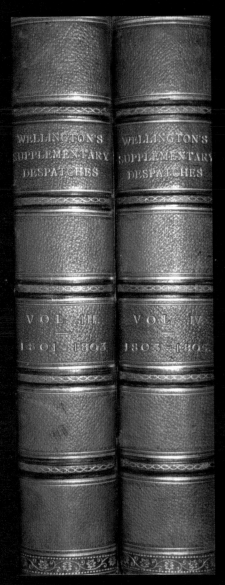

Douglas, John., *Douglas's Tale of the Peninsula and Waterloo*, ed. Stanley Monick (London, 1997).

Duncan, Major Francis, *History of the Royal Regiment of Artillery* (London, 1879).

D'Urban, Sir Benjamin, *The Peninsular Journal of Major General Sir Benjamin D'Urban, 1808–1817*, ed. I. J. Rousseau (London, 1930).

Dyneley, T., *Letters Written by Lieutenant General Thomas Dyneley, While on Active Service Between the Years 1806 and 1815* (Cambridge, 1984).

Ellesmere, Francis., *Personal Reminiscences of the Duke of Wellington* (London, 1904).

Esdaile, C. J., *The Duke of Wellington and the Command of the Spanish Army, 1812–14* (London, 1990).

———, *The Peninsular War* (London, 2002).

———, *The Spanish Army in the Peninsular War* (Manchester, 1988).

Farmer, George., *The Light Dragoon*, ed. G. R. Gleig (London, 1850).

Fletcher, Ian, *Craufurd's Light Division: the Life of Robert Craufurd and His Command of the Light Division* (Tunbridge Wells, 1992).

———, *Galloping at Everything: the British Cavalry in the Peninsular War and at Waterloo, 1808 15* (Staplehurst, 1999).

———, *In Hell Before Daylight: the Siege and Storming of the Castle of Badajoz, March–April 1812* (Tunbridge Wells, 1984).

———, *Wellington's Army* (London, 1997).

———, *Wellington's Regiments: the Men and their Battles, from Roliça to Waterloo, 1808–1815* (Staplehurst, 1995).

Fletcher, Ian, and Poulter, R., *Gentlemen's Sons: the Foot Guards in the Peninsula and at Waterloo, 1808–1815* (Tunbridge Wells, 1992).

Fortescue, J. W., *A History of the British Army* (13 vols, London, 1899–1930).

Gardyne, Lieutenant Colonel C., *The Life of a Regiment (Edinburgh,* 1929).

Gates, David, *The Spanish Ulcer: a History of the Peninsular War* (London, 1986).

Glover, Gareth, ed., *Wellington's Lieutenant, Napoleon's Gaoler: the Peninsula Letters and St Helena Diaries of Sir George Ridout Bingham* (Barnsley, 2005).

Glover, M., *The Peninsular War, 1807–1814* (Newton Abbott, 1974).

———, *Wellington's Army in the Peninsula, 1808–1814* (Newton Abbott, 1977).

Griffith, Paddy, (Editor), *Wellington Commander: the Iron Duke's Generalship* (Chichester, 1985).

Guedalla, P., *The Duke* (London, 1931).

Guthrie, J., *Commentaries on the Surgery of War* (London, 1853).

Hamilton, Lieutenant General Sir F. W. *The Origin and History of the First or Grenadier Guards* (London, 1874).

Haswell, Jock., *The First Respectable Spy: the Life and Times of Colquhoun Grant, Wellington's Head of Intelligence* (London, 1969).

Haythornthwaite, P., *The Armies of Wellington* (London, 1994).

———, *British Infantry of the Napoleonic Wars* (London, 1987).

———, *Uniforms of the Peninsular War, 1807–1814* (Poole, 1978).

———, *Wellington's Military Machine* (Tunbridge Wells, 1989).

Henegan, Sir Richard., *Seven Years' Campaigning in the Peninsula and the Netherlands from 1808 to 1815* (2 vols, London, 1846).

Hennell, George, *A Gentleman Volunteer: the Letters of George Hennel from the Peninsular War, 1812–1813*, ed. Michael Glover (London, 1979).

Hennen, J., *The Principles of Military Surgery* (London, 1818).

Jones, Sir J., T. *Journal of the Sieges Carried on by the Army under the Duke of Wellington in Spain, Between the Years 1811 and 1814* (3 vols, London, 1846).

Kincaid, Captain J., *Random Shots from a Rifleman* (London, 1835).

Knollys, W., *Shaw the Life Guardsman* (London, 1885).

Landmann, Colonel C., *Recollections of My Military Life* (2 vols, London, 1854).

Le Marchant, Denis., *Memoirs of the Late Major General Le Marchant, 1766–1812* (Staplehurst, 1997).

Leith, J., *Memoirs of the Late Lieutenant General Sir James Leith*, G.C.B. (London, 1818).

Levinge, R., *Historical Records of the Forty-Third Monmouthshire Light Infantry* (London, 1868).

Lipscombe, Nick., *The Peninsular War Atlas*, (London, 2011)

Londonderry, Marquess of, *Narrative of the Peninsular War from 1808 to 1813* (London, 1829).

Long, R., *Peninsular Cavalry General (1811–1813): the Correspondence of Lieutenant General Robert Ballard Long*, ed. T. H. McGuffie (London, 1951).

Longford, E., *Wellington: the Years of the Sword* (London, 1969).

McGrigor, J., *The Autobiography and Services of Sir James McGrigor, Late Director-General of the Army Medical Department* (London, 1861).

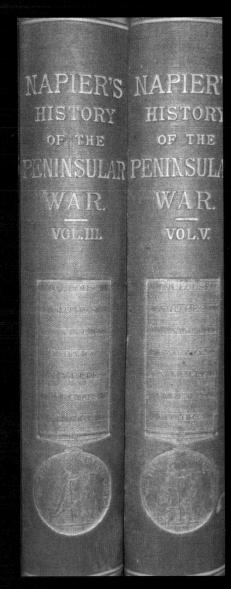

Mackinnon, Colonel Daniel., *Origin and History of the Coldstream* Guards (2 vols,London, 1837).

Maxwell, Sir Herbert, *The Life of Wellington: the Restoration of Martial Britain* (London, 1899).

Moorsom, W. S., *Historical Record of the Fifty-Second Regiment (Oxfordshire Light Infantry) from the Year 1755 to the Year 1858* (London, 1860).

Muir, Rory., *Salamanca 1812* (London, 2001).

Napier, W. F. P., *History of the War in the Peninsula and in the South of France, from the Year 1807 to the Year 1814* (6 vols, London, 1828–45).

Nichols, A., *Wellington's Mongrel Regiment: a History of the Chasseurs Britanniques Regiment, 1801–14.* (Staplehurst, 2005).

Oman, Sir Charles, *A History of the Peninsular War* (Oxford, 1902–30).

———, *Wellington's Army, 1809–1814* (London, 1913).

O'Neil, Charles., *The Military Adventures of Charles O'Neil* (Worcester, 1851).

Roberts, Andrew., *Napoleon and Wellington* (London, 2001).

Robinson, Major General C. W., *Wellington's Campaigns, Peninsula to Waterloo, 1808–1815* (3 vols, London, 1907).

Robinson, H., *Memoirs of Lieutenant General Sir Thomas Picton* (2 vols, London, 1836).

Rous, J. E. C., *A Guards Officer in the Peninsula,* ed. Ian Fletcher (Tunbridge Wells, 1992).

Sidney, Reverend E., *Life of Lord Hill, Late Commander of the Forces* (London, 1845).

Smith, G. C. Moore., *The Life of John Colborne, Field Marshal Lord Seaton* (London, 1903).

Southey, Robert., *History of the Peninsular War* (London, 1823).

Stanhope, Earl, *Notes of Conversations with the Duke of Wellington* (London, 1888).

Stevenson, J., *Twenty-One Years in the British Foot Guards (London, 1830).*

Swabey, W., *Diaries of Campaigns in the Peninsula for the Years 1811, 1812 and 1813,* ed. F. A. Whinyates (Woolwich, 1895).

Thackwell, J., *Military Memoirs of Lieutenant General Joseph Thackwell,* ed. H. C. Wylly (London, 1908).

Thornton, James., *Your Obedient Servant: Cook to the Duke of Wellington* (London, 1985).

Verner, W., *History and Campaigns of the Rifle Brigade, 1800–1813* (2 vols, London, 1919).

Ward, S. G. P., *Wellington's Headquarters: a Study of the Administrative Problems in the Peninsula, 1809–1814* (Oxford, 1957).

Warre, William., *Letters from the Peninsula, 1808–1812*, ed. Reverend F. Warre (London, 1909).

Weller, Jac., *Wellington in the Peninsula* (London, 1962).

Wellington, Arthur Wellesley, first Duke of, *General Orders in Portugal, Spain and France from 1809 to 1814, and the Low Countries and* France, *1815*, ed. J. Gurwood (London, 1839).

Wheatley, W., *The Wheatley Diary: a Journal and Sketch Book Kept during the Peninsular War and the Waterloo Campaign,* ed. C. Hibbert (London, 1964).

Windrow, M., and Embleton, G., *Military Dress of the Peninsular War* (New York, 1974).

Young, P., and Lawford, J. P., *Wellington's Masterpiece: the Battle and Campaign of Salamanca* (London, 1972).

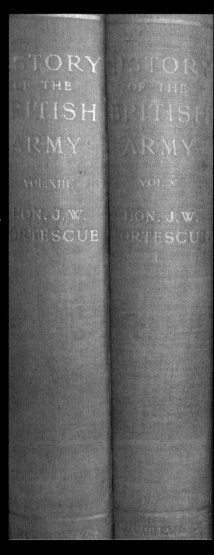

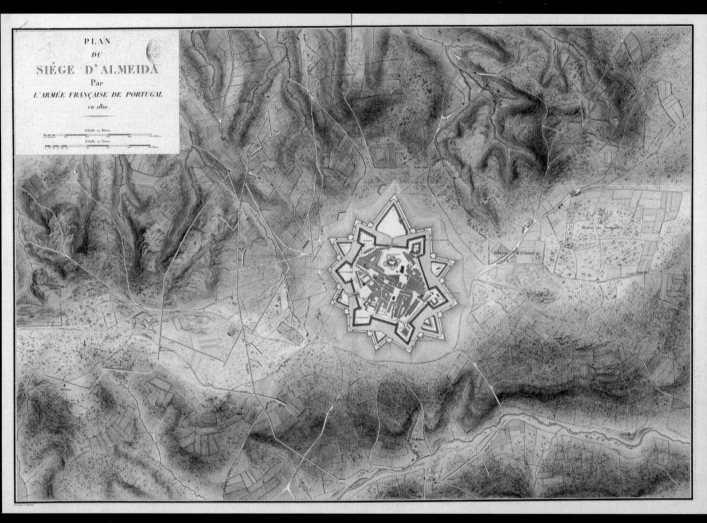

PLAN
DU
SIÉGE D'ALMEIDA
Par
L'ARMÉE FRANÇAISE DE PORTUGAL
en 1810

Two fine examples of French cartography from Belmas' history of the French siege operations in the Peninsula. Above, the siege of Almeida and, opposite, the chateau of Burgos.

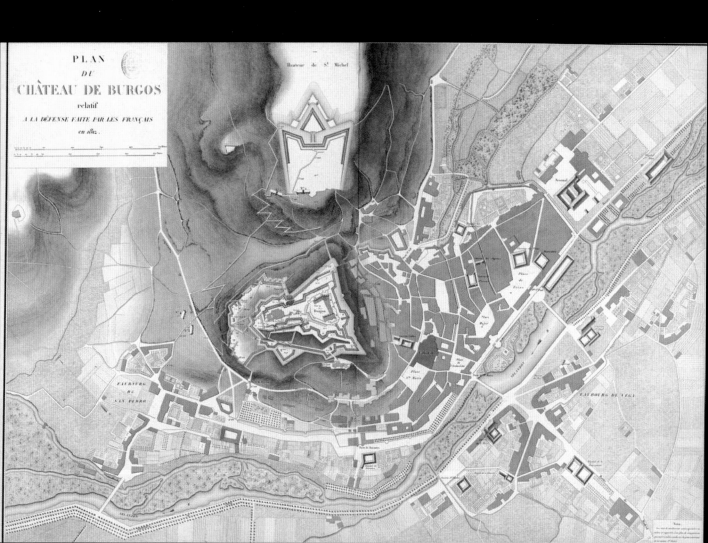

Ian Fletcher Battlefield Tours

Ian Fletcher offers fully escorted tours, not only to the
battlefields of the Peninsular War and Waterloo
Campaign, but also many other European conflicts, such
as the War of Austrian Succession, The Crimean War, and
Napoleon's Campaigns. All tours are accompanied by
expert guides. Full details from:

Ian Fletcher Battlefield Tours
PO Box 112, Rochester, Kent, ME1 2EX
Tel: 01634 319973
enquiries@ifbt.co.uk
www.ifbt.co.uk

DIEU ET MON DROIT

IN MEMORY
OF THE GALLANT BRITISH SOLDIERS
WHO GAVE THEIR LIVES
FOR THE GREATNESS OF THEIR OWN COUNTRY
AND FOR INDEPENDENCE
AND LIBERTY OF SPAIN

A LA MEMORIA
DE LOS
VALIENTES SOLDADOS BRITANICOS
QUE DIERON LA VIDA
POR LA GRANDEZA DE SU PAIS
Y POR LA INDEPENDENCIA
Y LA LIBERTAD DE ESPAÑA

Index